About Island Press

Since 1984, the nonprofit organization Island Press has been stimulating, shaping, and communicating ideas that are essential for solving environmental problems worldwide. With more than 1,000 titles in print and some 30 new releases each year, we are the nation's leading publisher on environmental issues. We identify innovative thinkers and emerging trends in the environmental field. We work with world-renowned experts and authors to develop cross-disciplinary solutions to environmental challenges.

Island Press designs and executes educational campaigns in conjunction with our authors to communicate their critical messages in print, in person, and online using the latest technologies, innovative programs, and the media. Our goal is to reach targeted audiences—scientists, policymakers, environmental advocates, urban planners, the media, and concerned citizens—with information that can be used to create the framework for long-term ecological health and human well-being.

Island Press gratefully acknowledges major support of our work by The Agua Fund, The Andrew W. Mellon Foundation, The Bobolink Foundation, The Curtis and Edith Munson Foundation, Forrest C. and Frances H. Lattner Foundation, The JPB Foundation, The Kresge Foundation, The Oram Foundation, Inc., The Overbrook Foundation, The S.D. Bechtel, Jr. Foundation, The Summit Charitable Foundation, Inc., and many other generous supporters.

The opinions expressed in this book are those of the author(s) and do not necessarily reflect the views of our supporters.

SEEING THE BETTER CITY

SEEING THE BETTER CITY

How to Explore, Observe, and Improve Urban Space

CHARLES R. WOLFE

ISLANDPRESS   Washington | Covelo | London

Library of Congress Control Number: 2016946741

Manufactured in the United States of America
10 9 8 7 6 5 4 3 2 1

Keywords:

Adelaide, Albany, Austin, app, Berenice Abbott, community engagement, crowdsourcing, cultural geography, digital storytelling, exploration, flaneur, Iceland, Instagram, juxtaposition, Kevin Lynch, Madrona, Melbourne, Milan, Nice, observation, Paris, photography, Place des Vosges, Raleigh, Redmond, Rome, Seattle, Situationists, smart cities, smartphone, urbanism, Urbanism Without Effort, Vancouver, walkable, wayfinding

TO MY MOTHER, ROSAMOND WOLFE,

—

who is all about seeing the better details in life

CONTENTS

—

PREFACE

—

We mould [cities] in our images: they, in their turn, shape us by the resistance they offer when we try to impose our own personal form on them. In this sense, it seems . . . that living in cities is an art, and we need the vocabulary of art, of style, to describe the peculiar relationship between man and material that exists in the continual, creative play of urban living. The city as we imagine it, the soft city of illusion, myth, aspiration, nightmare, is as real, maybe more real, than the hard city one can locate on maps, in statistics, in monographs on urban sociology and demography and architecture.

— JONATHAN RABAN
Soft City[1]

We all have within us the capacity to assess and communicate what we like and dislike about our surroundings, to respond with delight, sadness, fear, or anger, and to discover how best to improve the world around us. In particular, what—and how—we see defines the structure and context of our daily lives. As city dwellers, what we sense elicits emotional and intellectual responses about where we live or the places we visit that leave us wanting more after we return home. When crafting policy and regulations, and when making related political decisions, we need to do a better job of finding a role for our human experience.

This perspective comes from both my professional and personal experience. In the well-known essay "A Way of Looking at Things," architect Peter Zumthor notes how childhood memories hold "the deepest architectural experience . . . the reservoir of architectural atmosphere and images that I explore in my work."[2] While I am not an architect by trade, these words ring true. For me, advocating the importance of urban imagery is an inherited trait. My father, Myer Wolfe, was the founder of the modern Department of Urban Design and Planning at the University of Washington, and was an early urban design theorist in the spirit of Kevin Lynch, Allan Jacobs, and others described here. Growing up, I learned to look at cities as holistic artifacts, or reflections, of the underlying forces at play in defining the stories behind urban form and neighborhoods. I learned how the facades of buildings, if not demolished or destroyed, inevitably show layers that are reflective of the sociocultural forces at play at each era of building and renovation.

But, as I have described in the book *Urbanism Without Effort* and various articles,[3] it was only later that I saw the value of what I had unwittingly learned by osmosis as a child—on the job, as a land-use and environmental lawyer. Without realizing it at the time, I was the beneficiary of my father's sketching and his photography, which I often emulated in "monkey see, monkey do" fashion. Not surprisingly, he argued that these visually related activities played a critical role in enhancing the written word. "Visual material," he once wrote, "can make a contribution to understanding the urban environment itself, the interrelationship of society and environment, and the development of techniques for study and communication."[4]

The perspectives I inherited from him included at least three other takeaways that have spurred me to write *Seeing the Better City*. First, a key purpose of using photographs to supplement the written word is to "simulate a three-dimensional community as people perceive it."[5] Second, people's responses to these supplemental photographs may vary based on their cultural backgrounds and past social experiences. Finally, verbal communication alone is often insufficient to convey adequate information about urban space.

My motivation for writing this book and my desire to help people articulate what they see—both what is working and what is ripe for improvement in their cities—is based on watching residents and pundits respond to various facets of urban change today. However, across space and time, the human response to change is remarkably universal. Consider the familiar sentiment in Charles Baudelaire's description of the impact on the senses of Baron Haussmann's era of renewal in Paris that began in the mid-nineteenth century: "As Paris changes, my melancholy deepens. The new palaces, covered by scaffolding and surrounded by blocks of stone, overlook the old suburbs that are being torn down to pave wide, utilitarian avenues. The new city's coils strangle memory."[6]

Many would apply these sentiments to my hometown of Seattle, which is in the midst of tremendous, fast-paced transition and a great deal of debate about how to grow "gracefully." Discussions about issues such as transportation, affordability, housing types, building heights, and density are at center stage. The physical appearance of some city neighborhoods is rapidly evolving and often looks very different from what existed less than a generation before.

These physical changes generate articles about tall buildings, luxury apartments, and worsening traffic. Small businesses complain when construction or road improvements block access. The movement of downtown-only developers into less-privileged neighborhoods (based on available land and proximity to public transit) spotlights fears about loss of character and existing community. Seattle-based writer Tim Egan confronted the rising cost of urban housing with a dash of humor, questioning how Seattle can retain its quirky charm as home to people like Kramer, the inventive yet always broke New Yorker from *Seinfeld*. To quote Egan, writing in the *New York Times* about his fear of losing such Seattleites to unaffordability: "Could Kramer still live in my city?"[7]

In another 2016 column, writer Froma Harrop wrote a strongly worded critique—unillustrated—of luxury "megatowers" and their downsides, including wind tunnels, "canyons of pollution and heat," blocking of sun and views, and the displacement of affordable low-rise units by apartments accessible only to the wealthy. Harrop's anti-developer motivation was revealed in her closing paragraphs, in which she asserted that "residents have a right to determine the destiny of their neighborhoods" and she aimed familiar vitriol against wealthy land investors: "The real estate barons often call the shots in America's city halls. The people must tell the politicians inside that there will be consequences to ignoring their opinions."[8]

Harrop's call to empowerment and her conjecture about the influence of developers, however, assumes a mismatch between a high-rise skyline and a conjectural, alternative city form that she and her neighbors would prefer. But this hypothetical "city many want" is an empty proposition without an image of what such a city might look like. If, as we can infer, it is an affordable city of low-rise housing opportunities, then that vision should be easy for Harrop and her neighbors to show more explicitly, with visual examples that complement mere words.

When a building boom dramatically alters the historic rulebook of city life, perceptions, points of view, and policy discussions abound, and, of course, they do not all carry the same message. Competing interests present differing visions (often lacking photographs, as with Harrop) of how and where people should live. And those who participate in such discussions usually oppose rather than embrace change or suggest what different generations and income groups might want from places relevant to their daily lives.

More often than not, the underlying look and feel of locations frames and fuels the more public and sometimes contentious debates regarding policy and regulation. But, despite the ironic use of terms such as *view*, *vision*, and *perception*, meaningful and exemplary imagery of urban ideals is lacking. In my professional and personal experience, communication usually centers on words, not pictures. People argue about what they want, using words—about affordability, design flaws, or building size. But I do not believe that they have fully learned the extent to which they can observe and document surrounding conditions for themselves.

Seeing the Better City is written to prepare and encourage more people to explore and observe urban space, based on their daily experience, and then to record what is inspirational and evocative, what seems to work in fostering an equitable, livable city, and what does not. Based on my experience at home and in other countries, and after speaking with many city residents, developers, city officials, and media pundits, I want to help elevate civic dialogue by presenting a model for looking more carefully at city form and the myriad elements of primary city life. This model tells stories—through "urban diaries"—and can make a difference in how we plan cities, design their physical elements, and respond to urban change.

In the chapters that follow, I will discuss steps we can all take, with a little help and prompting, to observe and articulate the world around us. Throughout, I provide visual examples, explain urban diary elements, and relate other instances where similar efforts using pragmatic techniques are already taking place. Many others, like Jan Gehl and Birgitte Svarre, William H. "Holly" Whyte, Georges Perec, and Jane Jacobs, have also encouraged purposeful consciousness of surroundings through visual and other sensory means. This book follows suit, and

(1) it takes urban observation beyond the design professions, land-use application forms, letters, and testimony; moreover, (2) it melds the elements of "what we see" in an interdisciplinary approach that uses the best ideas from photography, smartphone applications, history, planning, architecture, geography, and anthropology.

Changing the conversation about "what people want" in cities will not be as successful if the people most affected are not engaged. I suggest a broader perspective than academic study, professional advice, or editorial views, and greater focus on the recipients of change. City dwellers will only actually see the better city if they feel more involved, regardless of their background, disposition, or profession. We should awaken our senses, particularly the visual, and move beyond conventional memes, gridlocks, and diatribes about urban change.

ACKNOWLEDGMENTS

—

This book grew directly from ideas in my first book, *Urbanism Without Effort* (Island Press, 2013), a shorter work that preliminarily outlined how urban decision making should reflect urbanism fundamentals, visual examples, and diverse urban diaries. I thank several people at Island Press, who over the past three years have encouraged more robust, complete, and practical application of those ideas—particularly Courtney Lix, whose editing skills once again kept me both humble and grounded, and Heather Boyer, who suggested ways to give new life and meaning to well-established ideas about urban observation.

I also thank my wife, Fiona de Kerckhove, and our children and extended familes, for their patience as this project developed and matured, and for their valuable real-world perspective on the urban places pictured here. Thank you also to several urbanist peers for their ongoing support of my writing and photographs—in particular, Kaid Benfield, Victor Dover, and Michael Mehaffy—with special gratitude to Lee Einsweiler of Code Studio for the *gestalt* we shared in devising the *Seeing the Better City* title in April 2015. I am also indebted to many friends, neighbors, and colleagues for their input, interviews, and overall inspiration. University of Washington professor emeritus Dennis Ryan shared thoughts and class materials from his long-taught "Reading the City" course in the Department of Urban Design and Planning, and several other faculty members, including Anne Vernez-Moudon and Manish Chalana, pointed me toward valuable resources. Seattle author Lou Rowan pointed to Charles Dickens's extraordinary capacity to put vision into words. As indicated in the text and notes, several others, including former Seattle mayor Mike McGinn and former city council members Richard Conlin and Sally Clark, shared their policy, regulatory, and decision-making experience. In late 2014, Professors Sergio Porta and Ombretta Romice, as well as PhD candidate Alex Maxwell, supported my presentation and application of *Seeing the Better City* concepts during my week as a visiting scholar in the Urban Design Studies Unit at the University of Strathclyde in Glasgow, Scotland. Likewise, in Western Australia, Marion Fulker and Fremantle mayor Brad Pettitt provided inspiration from Perth and environs during my visit and speaking engagement there in September, 2015.

Thanks also to fellow lawyers, such as Jessica Clawson in Seattle and Dwight Merriam in Hartford, who have supported my interdisciplinary approach, and the Washington State Bar Association and Colorado Bar Association for allowing several recent interdisciplinary presentations. Similarly, many supportive editors from 2009 to 2015 encouraged content that was later adapted here, including Sommer Mathis, editor of *CityLab*; Nicholas Jackson, former associate editor at the *Atlantic*; and David Brewster, Greg Shaw, and Mary Bruno, all former publishers of Seattle's *Crosscut*.

Final acknowledgment and appreciation goes to two individuals who helped inform and perfect the book prior to publication. Sarah Oberklaid, a Melbourne, Australia, urban planner, provided invaluable research and comments to the discussion of practical approaches and examples that otherwise would have been incomplete. Justin Panganiban, a concurrent Master of Urban Planning and Landscape Architecture student at the University of Washington (also my former teaching assistant and the recipient of a scholarship endowment in my father's name), added editorial insight and rounded out citations and definitions on short notice and with valued precision.

INTRODUCTION

—

WHY URBAN OBSERVATION MATTERS: SEEING THE BETTER CITY

The idea for this book—a "how-to" guide for organizing and applying visual insights about urban space—germinated one day in 2015, after I showed Meghan Stromberg, the editor in chief of *Planning* magazine, the dramatic changes to the skyline while we walked across downtown Seattle. Later that day, in a discussion about the role of photography in regulatory improvement efforts, some thoughts coalesced for me.

Lee Einsweiler, a planning consultant leading the team developing a new zoning code for the City of Los Angeles, explained how they were addressing the prospect of regulation for the areas between build-to lines and the street edge in certain commercial zones.[1] Citing Barcelona, where he noted that a uniform, repetitive building type nonetheless yields one of the most livable and visually diverse cities in the world, Lee suggested one option for Los Angeles was, as in Barcelona, to allow owner discretion about how best to treat lower-floor building facades and frontage areas.[2]

Lee then referenced the role of visual examples and how what we see, as memorialized in photographs, can evoke optimal urban solutions. He commented on a particular night view I had photographed the evening before, with human forms blending with an evolving skyline. (See plate 1.) "Your photos," he said, "show us what we want to see." We talked about "seeing the better city." And I walked away with a working idea, that photographs documenting urban potential deserved more attention, and could be an effective contribution to emotional, controversial discussions about urban change.

I recalled how recommendations of a regulatory-reform task force some years before had suggested that small-scale commercial development—like a corner store or a bakery—might work well again in single-family neighborhoods. However, in response to organized opposition, final legislation did not contain those provisions. As a task force member, I had always wondered if one or more pictures could have changed the outcome.[3]

Not long after my meeting with Lee, I discussed these ideas with former Seattle mayor Mike McGinn as he showed me the "best and worst" of his Greenwood neighborhood from the perspective of his decades of community activism, including four years as a big-city mayor. As McGinn underscored while in office, the two-dimensional language of government control—"comprehensive plans," "zoning," "lot coverage," "permitting," etc.—does not allow for full communication of the actual, day-to-day city experience.[4] His focus reminded me of many goals that Greenwood neighbors aspired to—visions, I thought, worth sharing with images as well as words, and in ways other than at traditional government meetings or input sessions.

After many years practicing land-use and environmental law, I have also found these modern-day regulatory approaches lacking, because, without more subjective observation and commentary, they do not adequately express our personal cities from within, nor equip governmental leaders to understand the multifaceted and increasingly diverse urban world. We also need interpretive tools to build on past efforts to observe and characterize city life, and to move beyond observation for observation's sake. Finally, "bottom-up" advocacy will also benefit from the use of well-considered visual examples facilitated by the processes described later in this book.

While we have specific recipes for the drafting of zoning codes, and tactical approaches to repairing suburbs and sprawl, we don't have enough guides for public officials to become familiar with their surroundings that are subject to policy and regulation, or to become confident in legislating many intrinsic elements of a successful urbanism. These elements were once summarized by Allan Jacobs and Donald Appleyard; they include deriving place from placelessness and retaining authenticity, livability, intensity, integration, and diverse public spaces and ways.[5]

As academics Kevin Lynch and Malcolm Rivkin wrote over fifty years ago about urban perception, describing the study groups used in their research: "Most of these people felt strongly about their visual world, even if they found difficulty in being articulate about it. . . . The look of the world did indeed make a difference in their lives."[6] Today, with readily available smartphone cameras, blogging, social media platforms, and apps, anyone can immediately express—and share—how they feel about their cities, and municipal programming and decision-making processes are incorporating new ways to engage and incorporate these voices.

I believe that everyone can read and document the city from their unique "urban diary" perspectives, using cityscapes and urban spaces as if they are words on a page. While some such pages emphasize our day-to-day interactions with people and urban space, whether at home, at work, or in situations in between, other pages feature more objective descriptions of relevant world trends or the local urban context, based on history, the marketplace, design approaches, or urban policies and plans. It is critical to approach urban change holistically, by better emphasizing, not just the positions of interest groups but what each of us sees and senses, and focusing on what the many aspects of the city look like through our various personal lenses.

The Heart of the City and the Rational Mind

Jacques Yonnet, a journalist-in-hiding who chronicled street life in occupied Paris during World War II, suggested the dangers of quick judgment about the essence of a city: "To get to the heart of a city, to learn its most subtle secrets, takes infinite tenderness, and patience sometimes to the point of despair. It calls for an artlessly delicate touch, a more or less unconditional love."[7]

Countless other references, often poetic and historical, have framed the setting of the urban explorer, and quotations about perceiving the city help prime the eye, pen, or camera toward their observational use. Author Luc Sante described the observational acumen of the Parisian *flâneur* as, among other things, "everything too subjective for professionals to credit."[8]

Such a sentiment about visualizing and assessing urban change shows how the very nature of our relationships to urban places inherently lacks precision. By contrast, day-to-day city policy, planning, regulation, and response may demand clear language and conclusions to move forward. My friend and fellow photographer, Seattle developer

Figure 0.1 Immersion.

and former Seattle Downtown Design Review Board chair Murphy McCullough, likes to talk about the emotions that surround changes to places, and the importance of finding a middle ground for reflective observation and discussion.[9]

When describing our changing surroundings, plain language often eludes us, and it is all too easy to slip into heady concepts and lofty theories about the relationships between people and urban space. What we see, do, and say about the city is ambiguous, and does not easily or logically unravel. As another developer once said to me, it is important to rediscover the lost art of simply telling stories—something I wholeheartedly embrace, with my added visual elaboration.

About Stories, and Words on a Page

Once upon a time, before data was organized to characterize urban areas and trends, people told stories about what they saw and experienced. Inspirational oral histories, myths, and creation stories were rich with imagery and often tied to particular locations and landmarks. They described the spaces where people settled, and where cities grew. Exploration, observation, and experience of place played a critical role for both storytellers and listeners. While modes of communication may have changed, our capacity to explore, observe, and improve the immediate world around us remains with us today.

Earlier in my career, I learned about sensing the history of a place from professional and personal perspectives. I participated in mandatory federal permit consultations with Native Americans for a lakefront professional sports team headquarters and a light-rail maintenance facility. Based on adjacency to a former village site and a sacred landform, I watched tribal council members and elders determine how these places were special by visiting them and carefully sensing whether significant stories remained in the potentially impacted lands. Within days, I spoke of this experience at a memorial gathering for a recently deceased friend, soon after spontaneously stopping in place while crossing a Seattle driveway where I had had a poignant conversation with that friend some twenty-five years before. I concluded that watching, and also experiencing underlying, sensed stories, were part of an authentic and often discounted method of understanding an urban place.

Every day, our visual sense defines stories about new controversial city-planning ideas, innovative buildings, housing conditions, historic buildings threatened with destruction or with being overwhelmed by the scale of the project next door, and new or failing infrastructure or public transit lines. These examples are all longtime, observable components of urban life. How best, then, to put our visual sense to work?

In response, I champion the camera.

The Visual Sense and the Camera

Carrying a camera is also now second nature given the almost universal incorporation of cameras with smartphone devices and the multiple tools available for easy uploading to the internet—a variant of the "elicited photography" approaches discussed in more depth in chapters 2 and 5. In particular, cities are finding ways for residents to report problems and request needed repairs, sometimes with uploaded pictures of the issue at hand. However, I do not believe that these crowd-sourced approaches, born of efficiency, entirely encompass the human capacity to observe and inspire. In short, reporting a pothole with a photograph can be very different from documenting the human experience in an urban space, even though both activities rely on sight and some form of camera. The distinction is important. Associated subtleties of perception and associated juxtapositions—among them, the overlaps of new and old, natural and built, big and small (hereafter simply "juxtapositions")—are addressed in chapter 4. For now, we should first emphasize how to cultivate our visual experience beyond reporting a pothole.

Planner Michael Heater is one of the few practicing city planners who writes about the importance of photography in cultivating the visual sense of planning professionals and urban observers in general. He has noted that in our increasingly visual and social-media-based world, "photography provides an opportunity to remember, wonder, inspire and create."[10] Likewise, Anne Whiston Spirn, a well-known landscape architect, photographer, academic, and author, has compellingly invoked references to our pervasive visual culture in which, ironically, our visual vocabulary is lacking. She refers to the potential of visual thinking "as a powerful ability, and photography one of its tools, but that potential is unfulfilled."[11]

Even before discovering Heater and Spirn's respective points of view, I was very aware that most of my peer professionals do not photograph with purpose unless developing examples to elicit client response or to illustrate reports. Yet I am seldom without a camera when moving around cities, both at home and abroad. I use the camera as a sentinel and, later, as a tool of detailed analysis to document and understand what I see.

I could not agree more with Spirn's sentiment about the missed opportunity to observe and learn with the help of readily available photographic tools: "Never have so many people owned cameras, and never have their snapshots been so widely distributed and shared. The world is being recorded, but to what end? *Few use the camera as a way to think*" (emphasis added).[12]

Others have expressed to land-use professionals the critical importance of having a camera available at all times. In a 2011 *Planning* magazine article, Randall Arendt suggested that planners carry a small camera to increase the effectiveness of the profession by recording "images of things that surprise and delight them and those that produce feelings of sadness or disgust."[13] His advice is relevant to anyone interested in urban observation. As I discuss further in chapter 5, many other city-planning efforts today use the camera, apps, and new online platforms to share photos and short videos online.

City residents all have stories about emotional responses to photographs of changing urban environments, including places that stir particular memories, such as a home. People react to images of new construction or changing ways to get from here to there. These responses, however, are only the first step. Consciously or not, we all craft our urban points of view from these experiences, and we should all learn how to express ourselves better and assemble these observations in affirmative ways that help improve both the experience of, and dialogues about, urban space and city life. I think the more meaningful and relevant questions concern how best to marshal the learning gained from urban observation, and how to put it to work in a verbal, technological, and crowd-sourced world.

Although we have recognized the same five senses since Aristotle (sight, sound, taste, smell, and touch), Yi-Tu Fuan's classic 1974 study *Topophilia* notes that human beings traditionally prioritize the visual sense over all others.[14] The results of seeing are initially dependent on context and perspective. I recall a diagram often used by my father in his lectures, which showed an identical image twice. With captioned, suggestive words, it looked like either a bird in a flock of birds or an antelope in a herd of antelope. Another classic example shows either two faces facing each other or a vase, depending on whether the perceiver concentrates on a central white figure or a black background. The lessons of these "negative" and "positive" spaces are not surprising; we all see, but "it depends on who looks at what," and from which angle of vision and surrounding points of reference the observation occurs.[15]

I agree with practical design gurus and art museum curators that "to see is to think," and seeing is a discipline that can be learned. I also value Nan Ellin's perspective from "The Tao of Urbanism" that we should focus on workable, vital, and inspirational examples (often the mixed and shared ways of using urban space) drawn from our specific experiences.[16]

Valuing the vital and inspirational does not mean that the "better" city should be beautiful at first glance, or immediately comfortable, or orderly. Rather, seeing the opposite is often more helpful to a more realistic, and holistic, point of view, such as the photograph on page 10 of a homeless person's tent with an ironically compelling urban view, usually reserved for expensive housing. While photographers such as Seattle's Tim Durkan often show pictures of the darker or less fortunate sides of civic life, such images often do not emerge until something has gone horribly wrong.[17] But we still rely on the value of those photographs to explain something to us, or to show "where it happened." We need to see the

---

URBAN DIARY EXCERPT NO. 1

*H*ere is one particularly instructive example of observation. One morning, just before opening time at the Seattle Public Library's downtown branch, I photographed one of the building's entrances, capturing an image that shows the inside/outside, subjective/objective role of a significant public building in my hometown. In the photo, I illustrate a well-known, central urban place, and, inadvertantly, I show how structure, contrast, and reflection frame and enhance examples of traditional human contemplation.

Figure 0.2

In his May 24, 2004, *New Yorker* article, Paul Goldberger wrote of architect Rem Koolhaas's library building as an "ennobling public space," lauding the return of a dignified, people-centric structure to the city center.* My image, taken six years later, shows several persons seated along the library's Fifth Avenue entrance facade. Rather than emphasizing the objective building, the scene shows people looking within themselves, pondering with private particularity, ironically reflected for all to see in the monumental public glass. In a similar photo from some years earlier, I show two people in a private moment alone with a dog in Venice's expansive Piazza San Marco.

As chapter 4 explains, we all have such personal cities that we can and should explain to others, and it is worthwhile to learn more about what they are and how they appear.

* Paul Goldberger, "High-Tech Bibliophilia," *New Yorker,* May 24, 2004, http://www.newyorker.com/magazine/2004/05/24/high-tech-bibliophilia.

These photographs show how we all participate in creating the city's image. *Seeing the Better City* is a book about the urban "without and within" that champions the subjective human experience in the tangible, everyday city, in the hope that understanding more will improve urban spaces over time. Later, I will build the case that our observations, as set out in sense-based urban diaries (filled, in my case, with photographic images), are our best means for successfully finding our voices within the visible built environment, and to realize, and then inspire in others, the cities we want to see.

Figure 0.3

stark contrasts presented by the "worst" city—or most irrational and intimidating city—to stimulate us to clarify our ideals for the better city, both as individuals and through a collective civic vision.

Both the public library (see fig. 0.2) and homeless tent (see fig. 0.4) photographs show more than assortments of people, a notable building, and an urban setting. They also suggest how exploring a city can show everyday inequality in the same glance that reveals different cities all at once. The photographs display the city of the less fortunate, the city of the reborn downtown, the city of iconic buildings, the city of the visitor, and the city of the spectator, or perhaps voyeur, to name but a few. Like the diagram that showed birds or antelopes depending on "who looks at what," a view of the Seattle Public Library's downtown branch or of distant hillsides covered with houses can vary based on the particular personal cities we first see, then capture and communicate.

Figure 0.4 Homeless, with a view.

Our Views, Not Others'

This book is not about the city that thought leaders and pundits tell us we should have or the city that others might want. It is not just about abandoning smartphones and observing solely based on technology-free wandering. Rather, it is about helping the reader compile and communicate his or her unique urban perspective through a diary approach that reflects thoughtful urban observation. The challenge is to probe and summarize how each of us creates our unique gloss on urban life and change, and how we arrive at our sense of balance between better and worse in our communities.

To compile compelling urban diaries, as discussed in chapters 3 and 4, we need a patient and interdisciplinary immersion. To further the earlier analogy, just as reading only one page of a book is unlikely to yield an understanding of its plot, learning to see the better city depends on more than a brief glance. Reading just one "page" cannot capture the core narrative of the city—nor the interactive experience of each person who sets foot there—whether based on themes of everyday experience, aesthetics, or feelings of happiness, safety, or security.

When communicating the personal cities that resonate for each of us, perhaps "seeing the better" city is actually "seeing the city appropriate to me." In my professional work as a land-use and environmental lawyer, addressing changes that range from new fences and new, larger buildings to creating more inclusive communities, it became very apparent early on that one person's observation of "better" may not fully resonate with the neighbor next door.

My urban diaries come from my cameras, and from views that are, at first, appropriate to me. The actor and director Orson Welles once said something similar: "I don't believe in learning from other people's pictures. I think you should learn from your own interior vision of things and discover, as I say, innocently, as though there had never been anybody."[18] I believe that Welles's self-realized point of view is key to the portrayal and comprehension of the urban environment, and that this perspective is quickly lost when one relies only on the vast array of stock photographs and virtual views available online. I learn about cities through browsing my own photographs—not others'—and from comparing images of similar human activities and accomplishments that I have observed in different places, starting with where I live.

A recurring theme in my research is how this process, or "art" of looking—which emerges from many fields—is similar to a systematic inquiry that others may term "scientific" or evidence-based. Humanistic literature, street photography, and the agenda of academic specialists in "place attachment" often overlap with more aesthetic or design-oriented rigor. Increasingly, human emotional response to place is at the center of cross-disciplinary focus.

In 1984, in an article associated with his book *Looking at Cities*, Allan Jacobs explained the role of looking in the context of broader, social scientific inquiry: "Looking at and taking messages from urban environments should be as important a research and analytic method as any other that we choose to use, one used in conjunction with others both as a discrete research act and as a constant part of our professional and personal lives."[19]

In my writing, public speaking, and legal work, I have often broadened Jacobs's assertion and stressed everyone's inherent ability to see their surrounding cities, over and above an interesting article here or an organized program there. I also frequently honor similar sentiments expressed by great authors, philosophers, artists, designers, and photographers. Like urbanist Charles Landry, I have suggested that the underlying sensations of city living should inform the dry language of policy and plans; we need a greater emphasis on observed, meaningful people–place interactions to help improve our urban environments and provide commonsense inputs about individuals' urban experiences.[20] Like designers George Nelson and Rob Forbes, I have urged more widespread visual literacy, however subjective, to elevate discussion and debate in the public domain.

Championing urban observation (especially through photographic example) is crucial because both support for and opposition to projects often depends on personal perception or visual simulation that results from pending urban change. Simultaneously, photographic applications, websites, and related social-network venues (e.g., Instagram, Flickr, Google Street View) enable virtual travel, filtered imagery, and augmented reality. When coupled with the smartphone, these tools allow unprecedented and immediate communication that can shape opinion and political decision making, as well as enhance questions of fairness and "who gets, who pays."

Most importantly, on a regular basis I suggest that friends and acquaintances, as well as clients and colleagues, take photographs of what they see. To me, our photography is the primary tool to influence the evolution of places that matter to us most of all. This personal effort becomes the biggest challenge: my city is not your city, as each of our perspectives is informed by our knowledge and unique experiences that are often underemphasized by today's political decision-making and real estate development approaches. What we see may not be what others see, but rather than blind acceptance, we can all exercise what Nelson termed "our varying abilities to use our eyes" in order to achieve "not any particular brand of truth" but to "enhance the possibility of uncovering many layers of meaning."[21]

The Role of Human Perception in a Data-Driven World

Almost every day, I notice new, visual summaries—such as photos, maps, tables, or graphs—that are useful to land-use issues, but they lack truly immersive and experiential underpinnings. For instance, a recent *Seattle Times* article showed before-and-after Google Street View photos of small, undersized houses from another era replaced in recent years by more-luxurious homes of greater value.[22] Another showed a before-and-after scenario of rapid change in Seattle's South Lake Union, resulting from a new live-work technology focus in a former low-density warehouse district.[23] In Mobile, Alabama, a Bloomberg Philanthropies grant has funded the use of Instagram photos to create baseline data to help assess and better understand and resolve instances of blight.[24] While innovative, these tools should not be mistaken for resources that give us a complete sense of the human experience in a place.

Planetizen, a well-respected urban-planning aggregation website, regularly reviews such digital advancements, including websites and apps.[25] Instagram (including Mobile's example) and Pinterest received high marks for their capacity to aggregate both visual inventories and best-practice examples.[26] As chapters 2 and 5 document, featured apps tend to favor service provision, data/information sharing and mapping, and simplified ways to alert municipal staffs about needed repairs.

The smartphone, new camera-lens devices that attach to smartphones, and readily available online maps, photographs, and data all provide visual opportunities that broaden the potential of experiential observation. Apps can facilitate how we gain and report our experiences, but our experiences are far more than mere fodder for tools. In the end, the human capacity to observe and process the experience cannot be wholly reduced to an app, as no matter how efficient or innovative the app's features and functions, our human senses still play a significant role.

Seeing the Better City celebrates the role of human observation. We cannot forget the innate look and feel that characterizes our surroundings. In an era of apps, platforms, data mining, and environments increasingly augmented by inspirational virtual-reality simulations and games,[27] we should consider closely how they can uplift and complement our own unique and valuable documentary role, still giving primacy to human senses that interpret the look and feel of our surroundings. Qualitative experience in cities is the basis for a populist view that will assure a broader perspective on livability amid change.

01 HOW TO SEE CITY BASICS AND UNIVERSAL PATTERNS

—

Although clarity or legibility is by no means the only important property of a beautiful city, it is of special importance when considering environments at the urban scale of size, time, and complexity. To understand this, we must consider not just the city as a thing itself, but the city as being perceived by its inhabitants.

— KEVIN LYNCH
The Image of the City[1]

It is possible for an inquisitive individual to take a hard look at ongoing change and then attempt to influence policy based on what they see. In Raleigh, North Carolina, Briana Outlaw, a landscape architecture student working as an urban-design intern, provided input to neighborhood redevelopment and affordable housing planning efforts by noticing cultural attributes of particular communities, and then suggesting that a sense of ownership in city planning efforts would be more likely if the city took a harder look as well.

Outlaw argued that if improvements were made consistent with observations of how space is used—especially roads, sidewalks, and old retail hubs—then reinvestment from within that avoids gentrification might be more likely. She described the tendency of the African American community to use roads as gathering places for community events, and asked why initial planning efforts used only traditional street and sidewalk standards. Outlaw presented her work in a study that included a paper and presentation based on her interviews, the meetings she had attended, and her observations around the city's College Park neighborhood.[2]

Other examples are less grounded in looking at existing conditions, and they tend to emphasize the sensational. In the summer of 2015, Danny Westneat, a *Seattle Times* columnist, described a leaked copy of a mayoral Housing and Livability Task Force Agenda (HALA) report that contained a series of recommendations about approaches to affordable housing types. Suggested modifications to specific single-family zoned areas included expanded opportunities for "duplexes," "triplexes," mother-in-law apartments, and detached accessory dwelling units. Westneat led a charge based on words alone; he suggested that the mayor's report would be doing away with single-family zoning at the expense of these more-affordable options, and before the city issued the report, these recommendations were taken off of the table.[3]

I am convinced that if the HALA report had contained residents' photographs of what many single-family neighborhoods already looked like, this debate about alternative housing types would have been different. To some of Seattle's mainstream media, images such as what can be seen in figure 1.1—depicting a long-standing small apartment building in my Seattle residential neighborhood—were entirely forgotten.[4]

Authentic human reflection should not be shortchanged by pundits' voices and augmented realities (such as maps, depictions, and overlays) that come from observers unfamiliar with the nuances of a community. As Brianna Outlaw showed in Raleigh, all of us, not just pundits, have a stake in urban change, and we should find ways to express our perceptions. Rather than contributing to the online comment stream generated by news articles, why not rise above journalistic characterizations of urban change by telling our more direct and compelling stories? As I explain in chapters 2 and 5, even Facebook, Google Plus, and certain readily available smartphone apps such as Instagram offer simple, exploratory opportunities to express our individual urban observations.

The Urban Diary Approach

One way of establishing context and providing meaning is through urban diaries. The urban diary is a method of observing and inventorying the essence of a place, describing a city dweller's conception of his or her urban surroundings, and establishing fundamental features worth preserving, replicating, or enhancing as the city evolves.

The premise of an urban diary is simple: cities are primary locations for human interaction and overlap with built environment features, such as buildings, streets, squares, and engineered parks or landscapes. The best way to experience and understand urban energy is to immerse yourself in these urban surroundings—and, in the process, record what you experience. Hence, these diaries are an important ongoing source of documentation and understanding, which can add complexity based on the senses and emotions involved. By now, it should come as no surprise that my urban diary has always been visual and, accordingly, photo-centric. However, urban diaries can take many forms: examples include a notebook or scrapbook in a binder, or a digital file displayed on a screen. Urban diaries can feature either narrative or figures (such as diagrams, sketches, or paintings), and like the excerpts in this book, they might capture actual events or record internalized memories or intuitions. They can include explanations of local history, culture, and climate, whether nearby or overseas, and note instances of what I have termed "urbanism without effort" (those latent, basic aspects of city life that occur without intervention or prompting).

An initial question about an urban diary is the locus of observation. Is the purpose of the tool to learn how to describe everyday surroundings, or to go elsewhere and decide what to illustrate for those back home who may not have seen other examples? I have found that the answer is *yes* to both questions. Is an urban diary necessarily nostalgic,

---

URBAN DIARY EXCERPT NO. 2

*P*lates *2 and 3 provide a simple example* of the provocative nature of photographs in the urban setting. At a glance, they show viewable factors—qualities that I imagine my father had in mind—of context and color, light and dark, land and water, nature and structure, where people work and live, and more. These first two images of Seattle in 2015 evoke questions about my hometown, but they don't need detailed captions or narrative. The viewable factors on display are all rudiments of what we see in an urbanizing world and suggest balances (e.g., between light and dark, or nature and structure) that are ripe for the ongoing dialogues of sustainability, climate change, the shared economy, and assurance of equity.

a way to document the supposed lost soul of space or place? I would say no, but I suspect many who are inclined to oppose changing what is familiar would disagree.

No matter the purpose of the diary and the sensory information recorded there, it is necessary to learn how to observe, which is not unlike learning to play a musical instrument. After mastering observation skills, some diarists may prefer close documentation of immediately accessible environments. For others, it may be just as important, or even more, to bring home lessons from afar.

URBAN DIARY EXCERPT NO. 3

Figure 1.1

My own "diverse housing type" urban diary of two blocks around my house shows several examples of "duplexes" and "triplexes" that already exist within a neighborhood of single-family homes. It is a *de facto* illustration of existing urban density that goes unnoticed, because, in fact, it has happened without incident or media attention. The use of such images could have elevated a policy debate over housing types to a more reasonable discussion because the feared "new" housing types were actually already in existence. Figure 1.1 shows a small apartment house that resembles a single-family home; it was legally permitted on my street some years ago.

In *Urbanism Without Effort*, I argued for returning to the "first principles of urbanism" in order to move forward with compelling, workable solutions that revert to a more naturally occurring relationship between people and their surroundings.[5] Like other authors and photographers, I have often referenced essential characteristics of the urban setting, such as corners and other sit-able places in the context of the "sit-able city"); such crossroads—whether intentional or inadvertent—are fundamental physical and social focal points of human interaction with the city.[6] The idea of "sit-ability" compelled several follow-up articles by others, perhaps because (as discussed further in chapter 3) these examples of convergence points—corners and sit-able places—offer challenges and opportunities worthy of study and contemplation, and as such are suitable initial vantage points for an urban diary.[7]

The goal is, to quote Jan Gehl and Birgitte Svarre, "not to recreate pre-modern cities," but to determine first what comes naturally—what could be considered readily observable, indigenous facets of urban settlements—and depict such first principles as a compelling documentary of fine-grained, on-the-ground experience.[8] The degree to which livability derives from cultural tradition is somewhat variable, but such organic urban development is readily discernable, independent of government intervention, policy, or plan.

I introduced the "urban diary" tool for urban observation in order to rediscover fundamental people–place relationships, and also because twenty-first-century issues deserve a holistic, experiential point of view. I suggested that readers, regardless of their backgrounds, can and should assemble urban diaries to help in the search for the basic patterns they notice in their day-to-day urban experiences, observed precedents, and desired social and physical outcomes. We need more purposeful *flâneurs*, direct observers distinct from "public life studies," mindful of cutting across the objective and subjective cities–observers who can articulate how they see the city change.

Figure 1.2 shows the power of pictures to capture innate urban knowledge. The urban drummer is savvy about where and how to place himself in a way that draws attention and attracts donations from pedestrians at the corner convergence point. City dwellers know the stages, windows, and observation points of urban life—the entry points to everything from transportation modes to safety at night. This book takes our urban intuition even further, illustrating how urban

Figure 1.2

diaries can suggest best practices for varied places of comfort, scale, and safety, with design and regulation provided in the public interest. Inclusive, observation-based approaches must accompany the printed word as authentic alternatives to the popular litany of buzzwords and trends.

Prominent forbears precede any foray into urban observation, and, along the way, I recommend several references. Jane Jacobs's simple allusion to urban immersion and participation may be the most helpful. Her lucid prose in *The Death and Life of Great American Cities* frames the question of the role of "Illustrations" in any observation quest.[9] Still, Jacobs's book, ironically, included none, and, as Gehl and Svarre have also stressed, she noted simply that "the Scenes that illustrate this book are all about us. . . . Please look closely at real cities. While you are looking, you might as well listen, linger, and think closely about what you see."[10] This often-overlooked passage is a major point of departure for *Seeing the Better City*.

Such snapshots of the interaction of people and places are what my father had in mind when he composed sketches and took photographs—what I like to term "urban mirrors." We can express these urban mirrors practically as well, in isolating the most proper vantage points to survey best and worse about city life. These mirrors show where the public and private realms intersect, frame the quality of the urban experience, and—most importantly—define the following

URBAN DIARY EXCERPT NO. 4

Figure 1.3   Figure 1.4

*N*ot unlike the two photographs of Seattle shared in Urban Diary Excerpt no. 2, the two pictures above show how people interact with each other and with the streets around them. I see them as the same photograph, one in Seattle and the other across the world in Arusha, Tanzania. They illustrate how urban observation can provide the fodder for interpretation of fundamental principles of urban commerce and transportation.

In particular, the images show different approaches to building materials, streets, sidewalks, and associated features, as well as, no doubt, different development costs. But in each setting, you can see an idle woman standing in a similar position. Familiar questions emerge from observation of the passers-by. What are the roles of commercial building form, function, design, and street relationship in each photograph? What stories result from journeys from home to work, and the locations between? What is important to retail settings in cities, regardless of place and time?

The answers to these questions help outline common baselines for urban observation. These baselines are common to all urban diaries—in essence, the parameters that we all notice when we look around our daily landscapes and bring subliminal routine to consciousness. To itemize them is to imply static characterization, but, in reality, they are parameters of interpretation in constant motion, cross-influenced by one another over space and time. Any photographic representation is, of course, a snapshot taken amid constant change and juxtaposition.

fundamental principles and questions surrounding city dwellers' urban experiences:

1. The boundaries of the built and natural environments inevitably ebb and flow.
2. Public and private spaces either separate and overlap with vitality, or segregate and deaden the experience of place.
3. Movement and settlement (land use and transportation) blend continuously. How can travel between origin and destination prove to be interesting, safe, and relatively efficient?
4. What is the optimal adaptive reuse of the preexisting built environment, with a balance of market needs with age-value considerations?
5. Traditional urban ways of life are returning; how do we walk, employ wheeled vehicles sensibly and safely with mixed modes side by side, share resources, and assure visual variety and a range of place-based uses?
6. How do we achieve comfortable and safe communities and neighborhoods, with related collaboration and protection (where necessary), without significant government intervention?

I arrived at the phrase "urban mirror" after seeing a group of men in Matera, Italy, likely on break from work, watching street life pass in front of them. Later, I read Walter Benjamin vs explanation of how Paris has perpetually offered the mirrors of observation symbolic of all cities "in a thousand eyes, a thousand lenses" focused on sky, atmosphere, neon, boulevards, men, women, and the Seine: "Mirrors are the spiritual element of this city, its insignia, in which the emblems of all the schools of poets have always inscribed themselves."[11] Benjamin's observations underscore the role of the subjective and emotional in our expectations of the city. In today's world, the vantage points that we choose for watching others are often the same places that we use to reflect privately, communicate with others in real time over food or drink, or communicate electronically with a cell phone, tablet, or laptop in hand.

Attention to these fundamentals allows us a personal return to the more organic city we have lost, which we must understand when we examine what bonds us to place today. As Joseph Rykwert explains in *The Seduction of Place*, these fundamentals still underlie the modern city.[12] Rykwert describes a constant interaction of planned and unplanned efforts of citizens, officials, and institutions. These efforts combine to morph the city over time, as globalization produces more and more of the random contrasts of vernacular building forms and more uniform, commercially driven building features.

Jonathan Raban makes the point even more dramatically in *Soft City*, his book-long meditation on the contrast between the tangible and the internal city—the built environment that we see and the emotions we feel.[13] Similarly, in his famous essay "The Discovery of the Street,"[14] J. B. Jackson evokes the first-person perception of the medieval citizen passing between buildings along familiar routes. Jackson issues a laudable challenge to the post-freeway world—to remember the importance of the first-person-based, organic landscape of neighborhoods, towers, and spires that was lost before we were born.

The Process of Sensing the City: "Place-Decoding"

I have previously discussed why encouraging people to sense and, in particular, to see everyday city life deserves a high priority in policies, plans, and project-specific, pro forma spreadsheets developed by and for our political leaders, planners, designers, and real estate professionals. Better cities will not come from a directed "see this" or "sense that" mindset. Rather, better cities are more likely to result if we first learn how to sense the city, understand which urban diary tools (such as photography) we should use, and then critically review or "decode" how people interact with urban space in their local contexts.

In-person observation (and later critical review through photographs) of this relation of people to their urban environments is something we can easily call "place-decoding"—looking at urban spaces for embedded and recurring patterns of how people have lived in a place for years, and sometimes even centuries. In my opinion, reviewing and understanding these patterns are the necessary prerequisites to developing future-directed placemaking principles. My photos, as interspersed throughout this book, have that basis in common.

For me, practicing place-decoding is often easier in parts of the world where physical artifacts show by-products of human settlement over extended periods of time, and cities can serve as "classrooms" teaching us how to realize our sensations and experiences.

While Seattle has been central to constructing the urban diary model, and Australia another influence because of its indigenous roots and dynamic cities, I have focused especially on France to practice my efforts to sense and understand the relation of people to where they live.

As *The New York Times* reporter Roger Cohen recently speculated about France's current struggle with modernity, "Nowhere else is the particularity of place and the singularity of a person's attachment to it more important."[15] Cohen aptly summarizes the French people–place dynamic and the relative ease of applying the urban diary approach to French cities and towns. In my opinion, there is nowhere better to see the Old World basis for the role of urban places and how they define who we are in the urban context. Beyond Paris, in the narrow streets and pass-through places of France's Old World city cores, latent answers to urban riddles await our quizzical view.

As the preface and introduction have emphasized, sensing—including seeing—the city is a personal experience owned by each person, whether resident or visitor. From a legal perspective, it is tantamount to an urban property right that transcends public and private domains. Our right to see, hear, touch, and smell the city is our affordable lease, easement or license that allows us to cross space and time and the organic forces of growth or decline.

But sensing the city is often manipulated or distracted by other forces, such as intentional design by someone else. Beyond decoding messages for future-directed planning and placemaking, we should understand encounters with the directed "see this" or "sense that" mindset (noted above) that occur in the urban experiential adventure.

Observing a place, photographing it, and then decoding the photographs are helpful supplements to verbal descriptions of improved urban space. These visual supplements inform goals such as increased public transit or bicycle use with a more holistic, experiential point of view, and they enhance our ability to sense the city and its internal people–place interactions, as well as to understand where manipulations or distractions occur. Additional apps, tools, and activities are helpful measures; I also suggest more "how-to's," such as community classes, meetups, school curricula, trainings, and, finally, sensitizing public officials and loan officers to the underlying human perceptions that influence real estate value.

URBAN DIARY EXCERPT NO. 5

These late-summer photographs show how place-decoding works in the historic center of Aix-en-Provence and at night in the small Corsican port of Erbalunga. Carefully breaking down each photograph shows ordinary human behavior and natural market processes under way—all of which might arise in the development of policies, plans, and regulations.

To me, the photographs suggest questions for urban planning practice and land-use regulation. Are setbacks needed to preserve light and air? How best to assure safe passage for pedestrians? How to honor the walkable places of the past, present, and future? How should a city enable successful interactions of private business and public ways, or create twenty-four-hour safety for street diners and children at play?

Figure 1.5

Figure 1.6

Figure 1.7

Figure 1.8

In sum, decoding these images suggests that we will not find the answers to these questions solely in the printed word, or in cookie-cutter approaches to urban life. Rather, such questions are the riddles of the Old World, worth illustrating and asking again, in places where their inspiration remains on eternal display—asking to be photographed, asking for rediscovery and translation to modern life.

The Importance of Urban Diaries and Local Context

I recently encountered urban exploration and observation from two different perspectives: first, my own broad-based inquiry in Paris, and then a city-led process in Redmond, Washington (see chapters 4 and 5). The variation in methods shows the range of strategies around urban observation and documenting what people see, as well as the complex overlaps of public and private interests when both cities and stakeholders attempt to maintain and improve urban space.

In Paris, I was on a very specific and personal mission to experience, photograph, and understand the human impact of a well-ordered urban space, the Place des Vosges—essentially the first modern public

URBAN DIARY EXCERPT NO. 6

*F*rench cities and towns are also good venues for showing the difference between a homogeneous, directed response to a place and a more self-realized, diverse place-decoding opportunity.

In Grasse, France, street odors are apparent and changeable near the Fragonard Parfumerie. Fragonard regularly sprays a variety of perfumes, as illustrated in the first photograph, and channels fragrance above a narrow, pedestrian street. Shoppers uncontrollably encounter the medieval, odor-masking reality that is perfume's very purpose. Decoding the photograph (with mist above) shows how a design-forced "deodorant of the street" manipulates passers-by. The urban observer must either depart or ignore the smell.

Figure 1.9

Figure 1.10

Figure 1.11

In a contrasting French example, the urban observer has free rein to sense and interpret the surrounding setting, without commercial manipulation of what or how to see. In the multilayered city of Bastia, Corsica, lines of sight span the ages and associated technologies, revealing small pockets of old that blend with the new. As the photographs show, different glances at topography present either an isolated hill-town setting, a traffic-filled city, or both. As a demonstration of the importance of angle of perception, one person may focus on the historic urban form up the hill, while another may see a roundabout of cars in another context, with little regard to the older church above.

Decoding the Bastia example gives the urban observer a better chance than does the Grasse example to sense for oneself. When the opportunity is greater, different people will see, or receive, different things, depending on their experiences or their motivation for looking.

square, and a precedent for many similar spaces around the world. In Redmond, I went downtown to the Old Town Historic Core, where my urban diary ideas were explicitly put to work in 2014 when city staff and stakeholders convened an "urban diary" workshop. The workshop was the first step in a process of addressing how best to interface this historic district with overall redevelopment downtown.

As a result of making these Paris and Redmond investigations, and after writing about the urban diary idea for five years, I see more than ever the potential for many different urban diary types, from diaries that create a personal way to know the city to those that result from a structured citizen-participation regime. Just as urban diaries may take various forms, they may compel different results.

While evocative photography and storytelling can bring home messages from another place, not everyone will view the photographs or their inherent messages in the same way. Similarly, local, stakeholder-based efforts to produce better cities are often complicated by motivations, perspectives, and ownership interests with conflicting goals. One person's desired building height and scale and massing to property lines may be another person's worst nightmare, or the perceived enemy of a historic building.

URBAN DIARY EXCERPT NO. 7

The context of urban observation and our particular experiences in and orientation to the city are all-important. The relevance of context becomes important when we begin in a vacuum, with only generic, visual representations. Without contextual clues, cities are like uncompleted spreadsheet cells where we personalize how space meets time. These photographs show how a uniform filter applied to multiple urban scenes quickly warps time and location, and obscures—yet somehow enhances—the reality of a place.

The simple idea of obscuring context with a uniform filter informs our point of view about city life. As noted in

Figure 1.12

the introduction, angle and frame of reference are key to what we see. When familiar frames of reference are not apparent, we tend to "fill in the blanks" with our accustomed values, perspectives, and belief systems. We can quickly assemble generic photographs that illustrate how we interpret uncertain, out-of-context backgrounds. Remove color, then crop, and leave only hints and nuance, and the city can become an off-trail place where questions replace familiar landmarks and clues.

Figure 1.13

In these photographs, five questions set the tone for this rediscovery process:

- When was the photo taken?
- Is the location clear? If so, is it because of personal familiarity with the place?
- Is the context of the scene apparent? What more is needed?
- Which element of urban life seems most relevant to each picture (e.g., safety, setting, transportation mode, the role of public space, public/private interface)?
- What questions remain?

What is the role of intuitive, human-sense-based experience in creating better cities? What is the role of urban observation? Can it resolve the conflicts like the one just described?

In one way or another, I have asked these questions of peer professionals (architects, planners, engineers, brokers, and lawyers), developers, elected officials, urban media specialists, and urbanists, and most agree that engaging the public and particular property owners in plans for change is key. As noted in the introduction, two developers referenced the role of storytelling and the need for "a middle ground where we can discuss the overall look and feel of the built environment and what we want." But another developer (who also moonlights as a member of a suburban city council) contended that determining balanced outcomes requires some direction; we cannot expect a local citizen to immediately know and explain what he or she wants from the surrounding city without prompting in the form of a direct question or proposal.

Whether self-motivated or prompted by a structured public-engagement activity, urban diary subject matter may not be immediately clear. I have often not defined or even been able to describe urban diary content in advance until I am inspired by what I see. Several of the examples in this book fall into that category, including the "riddles of the Old World" that emerged in France (Urban Diary Excerpt no. 5), descriptions and photographs of urban color and associated London walks (pages 67, 68 and plates 4 through 16) and a "teaching moment" encountered in Grasse (plate 21). Such observations made overseas, when compiled and presented in diary form, provide ready examples for local consumption and adaptation. Even an illustrated open narrative, without a precise conclusion, allows others to see, learn, and compare.

Urban diaries are tools of individual observation, which some associate with the removed, unnoticed, unengaged *flâneur*. Others demand more engagement in the act of observing, and see more value in "active input" techniques, with portraits pooled together as useful indicators of contemporary culture and city life. Active input appears on websites such as *Overheard in New York* (repeated quotations between identified types of individuals) or *Humans of New York* (brief biographies based on posed portraits).[16]

While there is a certain value in such approaches to engagement, compilations of immersion-based urban diaries also reveal insights into a side of the city not easily seen. Urban diary photographs might be submitted to organized city planning efforts or offered as testimony to local land-use proceedings. Chapters 2 and 5 address these potential, more-detailed uses of the urban diary tool.

02 OBSERVATIONAL APPROACHES

—

Experts may help assemble data, specialists may organize it, professionals may offer theories to explain it. But none of these can substitute for each person's own leap into the dark, jumping in to draw his or her own conclusions.

— GRADY CLAY
Close-Up: How to Read the American City[1]

As we continue to learn how to recognize the basic patterns of city life through words and photographs, we are increasingly embracing creative aspects of new technologies and social media collaboration. But recounting the experience of place, through relevant and enriching stories, remains critically important. We still have much to learn from inspirational authors and past approaches to chronicling what we see.

We can enhance our urban diaries with additional review of these immersion and explanation traditions, including several well-regarded frameworks for looking at the built environment. This chapter examines those traditions and frameworks, and derives helpful hints for their further use in urban diaries that record our observations and that might suggest ideas for improving where we live. Specific chapter sections also set the stage for later chapters that delve into the details of creating an urban diary. These sections examine the deep-seated lessons of particular spaces, the legacy of the storied *flâneur*, and contemporary urban observation and inventory methods. Some observational techniques discussed here require new technologies and apps, while others feature helpful questions and on-the-ground-approaches that help clarify what makes a place special or unique.

Moving Toward the Firsthand Experience

Grand and evocative statements about the romance of the city are often supplanted today with other catchy descriptors of urban identity. For example, environmental psychologists, authors, and artists all reflect on the interactive role of the built environment and human behavior with distinct labels for their work, or book titles that capture the types of cities they champion. Tony Hiss first assembled an accessible book about "simultaneous perception" and "experience of place" over twenty-five years ago.[2] Since then, books about how people can and should blend with urban settings have multiplied; cities are "smart," "happy," "walkable," and "people habitat," to mention but a few.

Many academics use words like *psychogeography* and the concept of "place attachment" to describe how we look at and feel about the urban spaces around us. Order is an important factor in human perception, at least initially, and some architects, such as Ann Sussman, stress that particular symmetrical approaches inspire a sort of primal familiarity. She suggests that, based on subconscious recognition, people are prone to a more immediate affinity with specific building characteristics that imitate nature—something that purveyors of classical and neoclassical forms already knew.[3] Charles Montgomery, in *Happy City* and his related workshops and "lab" work, has demonstrated how design aimed at fostering social interaction can create places where people are apt to respond more positively, to show empathy and collaboration.[4]

Some researchers have also added systematic ways of using photographs of urban settings, composed by residents. Resulting studies champion the tool of "elicited photography"—asking residents for pictures of what matters to them—to better illuminate what makes certain places special. Both artists and social scientists combine these images through "photogrammetry" and compile "data points" for representations of the significant relationships between emotion and place.

I suggest that nonacademically minded city dwellers, or those outside of the design professions, *do not need* these studies, exhibits, theories, or labels to learn, and internalize, how to look around. Scientific findings and thoughtfully interpreted data are not necessary precursors to our own individual and mindful efforts to experience and perceive the cities around us. It may be merely tautological to say so, but we are all human, above all.

In my daily reading, I have also noticed articles that pay only limited attention to the reader's visual sense, with few references to a visual vocabulary and visual cues. Articles that stress relationships of place to history and collective memory are also immensely popular, as are online articles that feature now-and-then overlays of city scenes, repurposing historical photographs in a way that is more than nostalgic to capture what city life looked like in a time of less regulation, with people more seamlessly blending in with the settings around them.[5] Photography of daring exploration of "urban ruins" garners much attention, and other provocative visuals portray realities such as the walkable city of homelessness—an underemphasized form of city walking that Seattle artist Iskra Johnson has described as quite different from the treasured "walkability" of young urbanists today.[6]

In the time-honored journalistic tradition, these articles are usually illustrated only by third-party photographs, sometimes taken by a staff photographer, but often from public-domain repositories such as Flickr or Shutterstock. Increasingly, blogging and social media platforms use companion photographs—only sometimes taken by the author—and they advance their ideas with visual evidence. I believe that using the photographic work of others is limiting, and not nearly as compelling as highly contextual, author-composed photos.

For example, Tyrone Beason's *Seattle Times* feature, premised on "resetting our inner compass," recently celebrated the virtues of technology-free urban wandering. He noted how lived, individual urban experiences on foot should not be forgotten, and do not need to be crowd-sourced. He explained how "urban backpacking," or aimless exploration of the built environment, should be a key facet of urban living.[7] In my opinion, though, Beason's "all about urban observation" approach misses an important aspect of exploration and observation: his article is illustrated by a staff photographer, not the urban explorer, and does not urge the reader to compile lessons learned in any way other than anecdotally.[8] By ignoring the documentation element, he neglected to explore the very self-realized power that his story enables.

The process of exploring inherently involves honing our visual skills and learning from what we see, both good and bad. A photographic record creates a powerful example for others, and it may garner more attention than an account relying solely on the written word. Before photography, authors such as Charles Dickens had to evoke images by the way they wrote. Today, most people no longer need Dickens's descriptive skills because, of course, the camera and smartphone readily reproduce a picture, often immediately uploadable with a short commentary for all to see.

A robust tradition of immersion and explanation is available to guide our own chronicling of urban surroundings. While others' essays and photographs may be instructive, improving our own urban observation skills goes beyond reading others' articles, or recording and sharing an image without reflection. Active development of urban diary skills requires continued attention to existing history, place-based learning, and frameworks for seeing the city.

The Immersion and Explanation Traditions

From time immemorial, people have recorded observations about urban life. Immersion and explanation have guided interpretation of cities in literature and the arts. Before today's technologies, human observation appeared through the pen and ink drawings and even older visual representations of the interaction of people and structure.

The Greek poet Alcaeus of Mytilene (c. 680–511 BCE), as reported by the later sophist and orator Aelius Aristides (117–181 CE), made human opportunities central to city identity: "Not houses finely roofed or the stones of walls well builded, nay nor canals and dockyards make the city, but men [sic] *able to use their opportunity*" (emphasis added).[9] In Shakespeare's late play *Coriolanus*, the Roman tribune Sicinius asks: "What is the city but the people?"[10]

Modern writers have continued to examine the human relationship to the built environment. Lewis Mumford and J. B. Jackson often described these human–urban relationships as buried—even lost—but discoverable through a core understanding of urban history that is more humanistic than quantifiable.[11] More recently, architectural historian and critic Joseph Rykwert has emphasized the personal nature and importance of the underlying, multidisciplinary urban dynamic.[12] Observation aimed at the humanistic nature of the city can occur regardless of the practical issues of politics, policy, and process. This type of looking focuses on the inadvertent elements of place and addresses first the human experience of passing through multiple spaces that is inherent to urban life. I have often noted Rykwert's distinction between the dictated certainty of ancient times and our modern experience with the surrounding city:

> The Roman who walked along the *cardo* knew that his walk was the axis around which the sun turned, and that if he followed the *decamanus*, he was following the sun's course. The whole universe and its meaning were spelled out in his civic institutions—so he was at home in it. We have lost all of the beautiful certainty of the way the world works. . . . [but] this does not absolve us from looking for some ground of certainty in our attempts to give form to the human environment. *It is no longer likely that we shall find this ground in the world which the cosmologists are continually reshaping around us and so we must look for it inside ourselves: in the constitution and structure of the human person.*[13] (emphasis added)

More modern references abound. Harvard Professor John Stilgoe is another advocate for learning how to observe carefully the built and natural environments. Stilgoe's most noted book, *Outside Lies Magic*, along with Clay's *How to Read the American City*, heightens the importance of individual interpretation of the city.[14] In *The Experience of Place*, Tony Hiss also pays special attention to the innate, sense-based "simultaneous perception" and "connectedness" of city dwellers—often in response to commonly overlooked elements of the urban environment (e.g., his oft-cited passage about the Grand Central Terminal concourse in New York City):

> Just walking through the vast main concourse of Grand Central Terminal, in New York . . . almost always triggers in me a spontaneous and quiet change in perception. It alters what I know about my surroundings and about whatever is going on around me, and at the same time modifies my sense of what all these things mean to me. The change—one that is reasonably known to all of us, or at least lodged somewhere in our memories—lets me gently refocus my attention and allows a more general awareness of a great many different things at once: sights, sounds, smells, and sensations of touch and balance, as well as thoughts and feelings.[15]

Significantly, Hiss uses this approach—and the importance of regaining the capacity to understand and practice it—as the basis for an entire volume on realigning the built environment with sensitivity to human-scale needs. Hiss has prefigured many of today's commonly accepted views; one only needs to review his essay on the once out-of-scale, car-dominated identity of New York's Times Square to understand the basis for its pedestrian-based reality today.

Even now, the most relevant examples of immersion and explanation may be found in vignettes that preceded anything close to an app-based upload from a smartphone camera. For instance, in 1866 Dickens said he knew London "better than any one other man of all its millions,"[16] and his work is well known for graphic descriptions of the sudden changes brought by modern life and lack of provision for the poor. Anticipating the cinema, his narratives barrage the senses; Dickens scholar Jon Mee has noted: "In fact, even while Dickens was writing, contemporaries found it impossible not to compare his imagination to the visual technologies newly available to them: the camera lucida, the sun-picture, the photograph, and the daguerreotype were all invoked as comparisons by critics."[17]

THE *FLÂNEUR* MODEL

Early in his career, Dickens became a London version of the *flâneur* and was well known as a journalist for his anecdotal portrayals of London street life in "sketches" that later matured in the descriptions that enliven his better-known fictional works. For instance, his "A Morning Adventure" (chapter 5 in *Bleak House*) shows his capacity to describe a London morning walk with photographic precision:

> Although the morning was raw, and although the fog still seemed heavy—I say seemed, for the windows were so encrusted with dirt that they would have made midsummer sunshine dim—I was sufficiently forewarned of the discomfort within doors at that early hour and sufficiently curious about London to think it a good idea on the part of Miss Jellyby when she proposed that we should go out for a walk.[18]

Modern urban observation also descends from the storied Parisian *flâneur* and the later street photographer, both of whom left behind still-relevant models of how to document changing city life. As the precursor of the urban diarist, the *flâneur* was more active than aimless, and offered discerning observations of physical urban change and socio-cultural consequences. In her recent book *Soul of Place*, Linda Lappin examines our "inner ecologies" through the *flâneur* example as part of a toolkit for writers on how to retrieve lost abilities to read the landscape. She casts the *flâneur* in modern terms as "an explorer of city streets, a keen . . . reporter of urban realities . . . the soul of urban consciousness and mass culture."[19]

Nineteenth-century Paris was a laboratory for authentic observations of multifaceted urban transformation as commercial interests redefined city life. Paris changed from a city of old bookstores and flea markets to one of shopping arcades, and, later, one of department stores; meanwhile, the mindful *flâneur* morphed from writer to photographer as the camera became a more portable, utilitarian tool to record change, showing remnants of old structures amid new construction. Author Luc Sante has summarized the *flâneur* as the recorder of the living city, a place of still discernable "ghosts."[20]

Figure 2.1   The *flâneur* recording.

In her classic work *On Photography*, author Susan Sontag explained in more detail how the *flâneur* begat the street photographer:

> In fact, photography first comes into its own as an extension of the eye of the middle-class flâneur, whose sensibility was so accurately charted by Baudelaire. The photographer is an armed version of the solitary walker reconnoitering, stalking, cruising the urban inferno, the voyeuristic stroller who discovers the city as a landscape of voluptuous extremes. . . . The flâneur is not attracted to the city's official realities but to its dark seamy corners, the neglected populations—an unofficial reality behind the façade of bourgeois life that the photographer "apprehends," as a detective apprehends a criminal.[21]

In his book *Walking Paris Streets with Eugène Atget*, Greg Bogaerts gives diary-like narrative life to several of street photographer Eugène Atget's photographs, and reminds us of the role Atget played in discerning both the physical city and all that surrounds it:

> Atget is often regarded as the first "street photographer." He was also a documentary photographer, his work giving us a remarkably complete picture of Paris in the late nineteenth and early twentieth centuries. By his intense dedication to his subject, he created a visual portrait of Paris that shows its culture, drama, poverty, beauty, and ugliness. Atget was an artist; his images are much more than "documents." They deliver a depth of expression and feeling that is seldom equaled by anyone practicing the arts, *deceptively simple, wholly poised, reticent, dense with experience, mysterious and true* [quoting Szarkowski, 1973].[22]

While photography allowed the *flâneur* to visualize and communicate in the manner of the evocative street photographer and early "urban diarist" such as Atget, the Situationists—an international organization of social revolutionaries and avant-garde artists that flourished in the 1960s—later transformed the *flâneur* to an even more relevant activist, critiquing the consumer society that pervades and alters public spaces as places to spend and consume. As a remedy, they urged city dwellers to avoid main paths, using the *dérive* (French for "drift") approach that Situationist theorist Guy Debord defined as "a mode of experimental behavior linked to the conditions of urban society: a technique of rapid passage through varied ambiances." The "drifting" *dériviste*, Debord believed, could reconnect with a more traditional, smaller-scale city premised on direct interaction rather than large-scale public spaces, and on "situations" (street spectacles contrived to shock the bourgoisie).

Atget's work, a perfect example of classic observation and immersion, suggests the importance of relearning fundamental human attributes of the visual sense, as noted earlier. The legacy of the *flâneur*, as well as currently popular writing by Rebecca Solnit and Alexandra Horowitz, is a valuable reminder of our inherent capacity to observe.[23] In the case of land-use professionals and elected officials, these sources suggest the potential for adapting observation skills to daily practice and decision making.

The urban diary discussed in detail in this book provides a further way to compile and communicate what we learn. We can, in turn, express our urban diary results in dialogues with friends and neighbors, and differentiate our views from what developers, city officials, and consultants may think is best. We can also provide inputs into the public process when there is an opportunity to do so.

LEARNING FROM PARTICULAR SPACES

Often, according to the *flâneur* model, the roving, discerning observer sees how the form of an urban space reflects an embedded past—a "psychogeography"—that carries lessons for planning and policy. Rediscovery of the backstories behind urban spaces helps both residents and visitors experience places in new ways. The urban diary is also an especially helpful way to decode faraway places full of traditions and memory that are not readily apparent at first glance. In these special places, the urban diary enables a more thoughtful and systematic inquiry into the appearance and arrangement of the built environment and how people have used particular buildings and spaces over time. Important factors include the shape of buildings, the choice of construction materials, and the reason for and shape of landforms and remaining open spaces.

Photo-centric urban diaries offer even more specific insight into places with visible cultural heritage and indigenous roots, such as the Native American permit consultation sites described in the introduction. At that time, it was inappropriate for me, as a lawyer, to document tribal councils in the consultation process about a uniquely shaped hill,

Figure 2.2   The duality of Broome.

or the mouth of a creek, both now within city limits. However, many years later, in Broome, Western Australia—on the edge of true Australian outback—I photographed the noticeable cultural confluence of Aboriginal and post-indigenous settlement, not as readily apparent in larger Australian or American cities.

Photographs of Broome present a varied, multicultural physical landscape that shows diversity in its form and daily life, with Aboriginal traditions and sacred places still abundantly clear. My photographs also show a readily viewable commercial history tied to the Asian pearl industry, cast against the activities of year-round residents and visitors. A more complete urban diary about Broome would also reveal a frontier town, a place as a destination for personal reinvention, with many ironic juxtapositions. For instance, the Broome Planning Department sits directly adjacent to Aboriginal land empty for its sacred significance, with subsidized housing for Aboriginals across the road.

Motivated by what I saw, I discussed Broome with others familiar with its special look and feel, including Australian vocalist Missy Higgins and her husband, playwright Dan Lee.[24] In their creative works—especially Higgins's song "Going North" and Lee's play *Bottomless*—Higgins and Lee use lyrics and prose as their urban diaries about a special place.[25]

Lee explained why Broome's uniqueness is visually apparent. From his perspective, Broome's built environment, and its growing community of artists, has historically included design reflecting place-based inspiration and pride. He emphasized that better cities are those that create processes that honor the importance of place. According to Lee, it is no accident that Broome is often a destination for people to reinvent themselves—what better place to create anew than a historic setting of indigenous creation stories?

Timmah Ball, an Australian planner with an Aboriginal background, recently illustrated, with pictures, the fundamental importance of now hard-to-discern indigenous traditions that underlie the city of Melbourne. After listening to dry presentations at an urban-planning conference full of words and digital technologies, she wrote an urban diary–like article.[26] The article interweaves photographs and text, and emphasizes how acknowledging the cultural significance of Aboriginal sites within the Melbourne city limits helps to champion otherwise unnoticed elements in urban settings and share these elements with a broad audience.

Without Ball's accompanying photographs, her explanation of the importance of rectifying a common Aboriginal experience of being "disorientated and detached in cities" may have been entirely misunderstood. Her images of significant yet partially obscured landforms in a built-up urban area show reference points for someone in search of a familiar cultural landscape.

Erin Tam, a consultant coordinating the public outreach for Seattle's waterfront redevelopment and planning, told me another story that bridges the roles of photography, urban diaries, a rediscovered cultural practice, and practical outcomes.[27] In this case, waterfront planners obtained a photograph, submitted through a regular "Photo Friday" citizen-involvement approach (an "elicited photography" example), and the outcome shows the potential for regular urban diary programming of the sort proposed in chapter 5.

On one such Friday, the referenced picture attracted notable attention. While not depicting Seattle *per se*, it showed Cambodian émigrés fishing for squid at night off Seattle's Piers 62 and 63. To attract a variety of visitors, these piers were slated for reconfiguration in a way that could inadvertently preclude this after-hours fishing practice. Significantly, the fisherman work only at night both out of tradition and technique and because, under current municipal code, the practice is illegal. From the dramatic, contributed photograph, the team working on the waterfront was inspired to learn more about what they saw, and, in fact, they undertook a pier redesign and explored code revisions to allow the fishing to continue. Critically, in this case the discovery of an "indigenous" fishing tradition through photographic documentation was the key connection to a real story and the route to seeing the better city based on the pride and sense of ownership in public space that Dan Lee referenced in Broome.

In another example, African-born architect David Adjaye noted a lack of awareness of African architecture when he worked elsewhere around the world. To offset this, he began to use photography from his home continent to document diverse examples in multiple volumes, often juxtapositional in nature.[28] Adjaye, like Ball, provides a form of a professional, photo-centric urban diary as a means to educate others working in the profession and to encourage a greater appreciation of both historic and new architecture, as well as the urban design of African cities. Consider whether simple essays on the significance of African urban design—without photographs—would have resonated to the same degree.

Finally, San Francisco blogger Min Li Chan cited an informative Canadian radio interview of Australian author Gail Jones, talking about her recent novel *Five Bells*, set in Sydney.[29] Just as Dan Lee and Timmah Ball center much of their work on the embedded indigenous past of other Australian venues, Jones focuses on the importance of an immersive sensing and understanding of more than material remains of a city's past, which she terms "defamiliarization." Jones describes "immaterial traces" of Sydney's penal colony roots at the site of long-demolished buildings, contrasting current tourist activities at these locations with the disease and destitution that afflicted the first generation of Australian settlers long ago.

Primarily, Jones attempts to bring life to a revitalized area by urging a new understanding of how its shapes, and spaces, were created by something embedded rather than tangible: "I'm very interested in psychogeography, and the idea that we must walk around our own place with an active intelligence and a degree of radical attention to what is there. . . . We ought not be the flâneur who is idly and languidly consuming the sights of the city, we must look at its shapes, at its motions,

Figures 2.3 and 2.4   Sydney and Detroit: inviting psychogeography.

attend to its sounds, corridors between spaces, the unexpected things looming up or falling away as we turn a corner."[30] Jones references Sydney's *Demolition Books*, archived photographs of former buildings in the oldest parts of the city: "There is both the *vertical* and the *horizontal* history, as it were, that we might attach ourselves to when we start to meditate on a city. . . . There's the history that seems to be unfolding and moving forward, and there's the plunging down into the interiority of the place, into its lost histories."[31]

In response, Min Li Chan urges us to see familiar places—not just places explored while traveling—with the lenses recommended by Jones. Chan provides useful lessons for today's observer about how to "experience familiar places in new ways" and explains how bicycle tours, as well as art, food, and local history events, are *de facto* invitations to "defamiliarize and rediscover everyday settings." In particular, Chan evokes the visual and speculates about whether virtual reality might assist in blending past, present, and simulated future views of a location all at once.[32]

Frameworks for Seeing the City

Urban observation, as stressed throughout this book, is not a novel endeavor, and we can learn from classical interpretations of how we perceive urban space, no matter the era.[33] Where appropriate, I mention throughout this book many sources of prior, sometimes exhaustive work of value to today's urban diarist. The summary below recounts three of the most important lessons from design professionals.

First, when we look at urban spaces, we maintain an unconscious search for order and familiarity. Second, the experience of passing through such spaces is a critical element of exploration, worthy of a close, ongoing look. Finally, a syntax, or language of form, underlies urban neighborhoods as a "code" that might be addressed by more formal regulation.

In "A Walk Around the Block," an article early in his career, Kevin Lynch conducted research aimed at determining what ordinary people see in their daily landscapes. He and fellow researchers set the stage for his later *The Image of the City* by breaking down the role of spatial qualities; the character, location, and prominence of buildings; pavement width and texture; color; vegetation; light; and other physical processes. Lynch found something instructive to the urban diarist: that we seek order or significant patterns in the urban landscape, either from ready-made building categories or patterns, or from something familiar: "The individual must perceive his environment as an ordered pattern, and is constantly trying to inject order into his surroundings, so that all of the relevant perceptions are joined one to the other."[34]

Gordon Cullen's work also addresses ordered patterns and itemizes features of the urban landscape. Cullen remains an essential reference to today's urban diarist, particularly his attention to the "serial vision" that humans experience while moving through an urban place. In *The Concise Townscape*, Cullen deciphered classic "townscape" elements and used black-and-white photography of urban places to define an observable "art of relationship" in the urban setting.[35] Cullen's many examples comprise an atlas of the "art of the environment" and provide seemingly countless illustrated definitions of urban characteristics.

Edmund Bacon's *Design of Cities* also contributed a direct, well-illustrated approach to reading the built environment, premised on self-perception and relationship, or "involvement" with buildings and spaces.[36] Bacon, like Cullen, essentially shows any aspiring urban diarist how to explore, how to observe and categorize what we do as we move through our surroundings and the places we visit. Through simplified graphics and text, Bacon illustrates classical design principles, from their ancient roots through more modern applications.

Figure 2.5   Corsican serial vision.

One photo-filled example—similar to Cullen's "serial vision"—is an important reference for anyone assembling a "linear pathway" type of urban diary in a less-dense-to-more-dense setting. Through a sequence of pictures taken on the Italian island of Ischia, Bacon's camera follows a woman delivering hay to the town of Panza; we see the colors, building forms, and textures change as the town grows closer. Bacon describes how these changing colors and architectural elements create the "anticipation" of approaching the town center and how "fulfillment" occurs upon entry to a small square with a church stairway and bell tower in plain view.

The woman's journey concludes at one house that emphasizes the innate, contextual skills of the local designer, who placed doors and windows, and used color, in custom ways appropriate to the location, amplifying the pathway experience: "This phenomenon, often disparagingly referred to as 'intuitive,' actually represents a process so complex—simultaneously employing such a range of factors brought into mutual interaction—that no computer yet conceived by man, or ever to conceived by man, can come close to duplicating it."[37] Bacon's example also shows how exploration and observation yield important backstories about community appearance. In this case, the dynamic experience of entering a town depended on a person's intuitive skills implemented long before today's technological innovations.

Finally, for any urban diarist documenting urban space and looking for common, underlying patterns, Anne Mikoleit and Moritz Pürckhauer's *Urban Code* is a not-to-be-overlooked attempt to derive a "syntax" from multiple scenes and infer "unwritten laws" of city life.[38] In a book-length urban diary, Mikoleit and Pürckhauer look carefully at a surrounding neighborhood and the behaviors that occur there. The authors offer a shorthand summary, consisting of black-and-white photos and diagrams, of 100 lessons derived from observations in New York City's SoHo district, with conclusions based on the principles of Jane Jacobs, Kevin Lynch, and Christopher Alexander. Drawing conclusions such as "safe surroundings increase profits" and "buildings outlive uses," the authors "encourage a way of 'seeing' into [daily scenes]— to understand the forces that shape a place, and how these forces lead to the creation of a special atmosphere." Some of their 100 conclusions provide an illustrated catalog of potential urban diary subject matter, which the authors suggest testing in other cities.

The Urban Diary and Evolving Tools

As discussed previously, both creation stories and "place attachment" are important aspects of the human relationship to particular spaces in a city. I have also alluded to the idea of "place memory" and sensing why a given location is significant. Throughout this book, I use words such as "remnants," "artifacts," and "ghosts" that evoke something less than tangible that nonetheless affects us profoundly. Remembering and relaying these concepts is a time-honored tradition and an elemental aspect of an urban diary.

"Now and then" contrasts are universal, both in prose and photography, as a sort of mirror that allows us to share how and why a place has changed. A standard approach is photobooks or online websites about a city or cities, with comparative photographs or transparent overlays of historical aerial views or significant public places. For years, the *Seattle Times* has featured regular "Now and Then" articles by Paul Dorpat and Jean Sherrard.[39] Another is a "Lost ———" theme, which includes a collection of a city's now-demolished buildings still visible in historical photographs. These photos are essential for developing the visual language stressed here.

Equally instructive are collections of contributed memories that explain why a particular place, often no longer present, has been relevant to an individual or groups, and is portrayed as a distinctly human narrative of words, or more. Seattle editor Jaimee Garbacik has produced an instructive example, *Ghosts of Seattle Past*—a collection premised on the city's rapid pace of change.[40] In *Ghosts*, Garbacik's curated, multigenerational cross-section of memoirs, interviews, cartoons, and photographs (disclosure: I was a contributor) is a one-stop way to review a neighborhood-by-neighborhood record of prescient memories that survive actual physical space.

Garbacik is both ethnographer and manager of the ideas I have embraced elsewhere: that places survive differently, and that the embedded memories of a city—and the vast array of its constituents—still matter. She is not random in her technique and has solicited (through press releases, community bulletin board notices, social media outlets, targeted media, individual pitches, and more) messages that she suspects have been awaiting attention. She recently explained to me that "the goal was always to be as inclusive as possible, to gather voices from as many demographics and communities as there are in the city." One solicitation tool was the simple notecard, and she left many in libraries, nonprofit organization offices, community centers, and cafés: "The notecards included our contact information and invited any and everyone to submit essays, art, comics, and photography commemorating places they loved and missed. We gathered hundreds of submissions in this fashion. . . . In interviews, we didn't ask pointed questions but instead invited people to tell us stories and reminisce. We told everyone we knew that we wanted to talk to anyone interested in speaking to us. We wanted everyone's point of view."[41]

The significance of Garbacik's project lies as much in the pent-up demand to be heard as in the substance of the responses themselves. I asked Garbacik what she learned that would be relevant to *Seeing the Better City* and to encouraging people to explore, observe, and speak from within; she replied, "We approached the curation of *Ghosts of Seattle Past* as a community art project, a collection of storytelling and cartography that we crowd-sourced in a variety of ways, both analog and digital. We began by establishing a web portal with Google Map plug-ins, where people could pin places in Seattle that they describe as lost in their lifetime. They were encouraged to include their memories, as well as what the restaurant, shop, venue, institution, or gathering place meant to them and the city at large."[42] As Samantha Updegrave states in her foreword to the *Ghosts of Seattle Past*:

> This anthology aspires to go beyond the confines of
> commemoration, as curator Jaimee Garbacik says, to provide a
> "framework for how our memories can inform development in the
> future." The root of the word *memory* is *memoir*, "mindful of." The
> act of committing our memories to the page creates a sort of folk
> history, the people's view that joins our past, present, and future.
> The pages are comprised of our memories of "times when," the
> places and the people we were. Its power lies in the amalgamation
> of our stories and renderings; when collected together they form a
> whole.[43]

Garbacik's range of participants is critical to the project. The array of contributions brings together a foundational interview with Ken Workman, the great-great-great-grandson of Chief Seattle himself, with musicians', writers', a lawyer's, and many others' views of restaurants, theaters, coffeehouses, clubs, and even a laundromat. The result is a resource for understanding the human qualities that define a place, but are often lost, not only to redevelopment but also to the dry language and approaches of policy and regulation, data and design. In 2016, *Ghosts* was being extensively toured as "maps, art, and anthology-in-progress," and was planned for publication in three editions: one in the form of the original, hand-made anthology, another as an affordable paperback, and a third as a freely distributed "zine" in order to reach people in a variety of creative, accessible ways.

Web, Social Media, and Smartphone Apps

New technologies can help urban observers focus on details within the city, and make more careful, well-informed observations. Certain smartphone apps have combined photography, wayfinding, digital storytelling, and other features to redefine how our perceptions are communicated. Chapter 5 shows what many cities are already doing to capture this trend and put it to work in the policy, planning, and regulatory arenas.

A further introduction to these digital tools appears below, with summaries for urban diarists interested in camera emulators, walkability, wandering, mapping, digital storytelling, and more complex approaches to place assessment. Web applications, social media, and apps also provide ways to experiment with urban observation and photography while learning more about specific interests and desired approaches. They can provide structure and ideas for urban diary techniques and subject matter. Several apps can both substitute for conventional cameras and integrate the process of immediate image sharing.

THE ROLE OF CAMERA EMULATORS

For the urban diarist without a conventional camera, Hipstamatic is a leading application of "iPhoneography" and it immediately expands the potential of the smartphone to mimic and achieve many of the capabilities of photographic traditions.[44] Its principal purpose, as a platform to emulate technologies, also provides features useful to urban observation and contemporary neighborhood redevelopment that emphasize "grit" and adaptive reuse. Among its pay-to-upgrade features are film styles and techniques valuable in former industrial cities and frequently used by street photographers. In one such case, the Manchester "Hip-stapak" is premised on capturing an urban look and feel through the architectural styles and "grit" of Manchester, England: "The Manches-ter Hipstapak comes with a new lens, Smith, and a film, Cheshire. The combination of both elements plunges Hipstamatic into a vintage atmo-sphere, mainly due to the prominent frame. . . . The result shows verti-cal streaks and a somewhat blurry effect, obviously going for the 'old and ravaged by time' effect."[45]

WALKABILITY APPS AND OTHER APPROACHES
FOR THE URBAN DIARIST

For an emphasis on framing an urban diary walk, QuizTrail is an app that allows creation and uploading of a walking trail anywhere in the world.[46] After uploading, users can follow trails by answering questions at each descriptive trail point before advancing to the next one. Users can charge for use of each trail or allow free downloads. From an urban diary perspective, such apps are of value if they lead others to suitable photographic vantage points or allow uploading of photographs to illustrate trail views. Recently, Leica Store City, in London, used Quiz-Trail to "draw participants into the detail of what they can see around them—perhaps views they have seen many times, but have never really considered from a photographic perspective."[47]

Similar to QuizTrail, Walc is a straightforward walkability app, allowing for navigation by waypoints and landmark references.[48] Walc claims to be "the first navigation app built by walkers for walkers"; it uses businesses and landmarks, rather than street names, as the basis for turn-by-turn navigation. Walc is user-driven, designed to evolve with increased use. Future versions will identify sidewalk hazards, user tips, and shortcuts.

Other apps emphasize indirect wandering. Likeways is an app by Martin Traunmueller, a PhD candidate at University College London's Intel Collaborative Research Institute for Sustainable Connected Cit-ies.[49] Likeways also attempts to entice the user away from direct routes in order to cultivate the power of exploration and observation. At the time of writing, Likeways relied on Facebook Places and compiled "likes" to generate indirect routes close to restaurants, pubs, shops,

Figure 2.6   Apps and photos at work.

museums, or art galleries. Currently, there is no integrated smartphone camera option, so while the app compels exploration, it does not allow for the next steps of discovery other than ongoing participation. However, Likeways is one example of an approach, still in its infancy, that may lead users to see their better cities, but one that does not yet provide the communication element so essential here.

Another app integrates wandering and photography, and emulates the Parisian Situationist at work. Drift is an intriguing attempt to digitize learning from Situationist Guy Debord's *dérive* ("drift"), guiding the user around the city with directions and instructing where to take photographs along the way. The results are stored for later e-mailing, blogging, or tweeting. Broken City Lab, Drift's developers, have described the app concisely: "Drift helps you get lost in familiar places by guiding you on a walk using randomly assembled instructions. Each instruction will ask you to move in a specific direction and, using the compass, look for something normally hidden or unnoticed in our everyday experiences."[50]

Other participatory mapping apps are relevant to urban observation, diary documentation, and storytelling. One such app, Where in Wally, provided a tagged map of treasured places and spaces along an "art trail" in Walthamstow (a suburb of London) for use by the London Festival of Architecture. Locations were accompanied by stories (often personal) about why the indicated places were special to the user.[51]

The Mappiness app introduces emotional responses to participatory mapping.[52] Mappiness plots happiness as affected by local environments across the United Kingdom. This iPhone app contacts each user once (or more) per day to anonymously inquire as to mood, location, and activity. The app responds with GPS data, an optional photo, and noise-level measurement. The goal of Mappiness is to determine how people's happiness is affected by factors of their local environment such as pollution. Mappiness is just one of many examples of social-science- or art-based attempts—also termed "citizen engagement," and "tactical" or "crowd-sourced" efforts—to aggregate, assess, and represent the emotional response to place. In all such efforts, photography can play a crucial role.

ASSESSMENT TOOLKITS AND DIGITAL STORYTELLING

A treasure trove of more direct documentation techniques already exists as integrated digital mapping and narrative photography, as well as audio-recorded approaches.[53]

For example, Placecheck.info is a group-oriented UK website that helps self-organizing neighborhoods assess what is unique about their localities; it offers suggestions relating to further assessment and organizing, establishing neighborhood boundaries, identifying critical issues, framing local character, and identifying the potential and location for targeted development.[54] The site contains several helpful guides on how to use generated information as a basis for achieving change, both through formal and informal neighborhood planning processes and policy. With the initial "walkabout" assessment tool and further straightforward guidance documents, users are called upon to look hard at their communities and educate themselves about other people, programs, approaches, and tools that can further improvements to the places they live.

For the beginning urban diarist, Placecheck's Walkabout is a good start, one that is similar to rudimentary approaches to urban diaries, no matter the media used.[55] Its basic list of prompts is worth reproducing here as one more comprehensive set of parameters for urban observation,[56] especially if enhanced by the use of a camera:

A special place

- What makes this place special or unique?
- Why does it look the way it does?
- What local activities or events have made it like this?
- Why do we like this place?
- What can we make more of?
- What potential is there to enhance the place?

A well-connected, accessible, and welcoming place

- How accessible is the place? What limits how easy it is to get around?
- How welcoming is the place? Does anything make it confusing?
- How well does the parking work?
- How can the place be made more accessible and more welcoming?

A safe and pleasant place

- What makes this place—and its street(s) and public spaces—safe and pleasant?
- What detracts from that?
- How successful are the streets and spaces underfoot? What could be improved?
- How can the place be made safer and more pleasant?
- How do people enjoy nature here? What is missing?

A planet-friendly place

- What makes this place planet-friendly? How are scarce resources wasted?

- How does movement use resources?
- How is waste handled?
- How is energy used in buildings?
- How adaptable is the place?
- What other features makes the place planet-friendly?
- How could the place make better use of resources?

Most importantly, a more applied set of Placecheck prompts addresses a range of criteria, including landscapes and natural features, buildings, street types, public spaces, shapes, scales, and public art.[57] Prompts also reference connectedness with the rest of the city and available modes of travel, as well as adaptability, and health and safety considerations. The website also provides detailed examples of specific British walkabouts.[58]

Other related "digital storytelling" approaches worth investigating include Photowalk and Soundwalk, which provide opportunities to move virtually from place to place while continuing along a timeline, a thematic narrative, or a story plot.[59] Storymap is often used by major media outlets as a way to complement news stories or as a free-standing feature, but is publicly available and anyone with a Google account can quickly assemble a Storymap presentation.[60] The Storymap platform allows a blog-like approach, with simultaneous and integrated words, maps, and pictures giving context and, by digital analogy to Tony Hiss, providing a virtual form of simultaneous perception.[61]

Finally, neighborhood group members may like the activist tone of the Urban Storytellers website. The site focuses on storytelling-based approaches, but more in the context of citizen planners, and it provides both rationale and "how-to" lessons for the diarist-reader through the "Your Story Goes Here" teaching kit.[62] The authors' premise is very similar to that of the urban diary construct set out in *Seeing the Better City*, centered on web-based multimedia and guided by initial questions of "How does the design of a city affect your life?" and "What are the mechanisms for you to affect change in your local area in terms of city building?"[63]

Assessment toolkits and digital storytelling efforts are notable for their use of observation as a starting point for improving urban areas. Their methodology is similar to an urban diary by referencing human senses, but, as "group-think" exercises, they often do not focus on the core, personal impressions encouraged here. I generally endorse these tools—at least as examples, but only if participants also compile personal and visual urban diaries, as set out in chapters 3 and 4, ripe for merger with other visual urban diaries—prior to any community-organization effort such as Placecheck.

THE DEVELOPING DIGITAL IMPACT OF THE URBAN DIARY

Finally, for those interested in how others are adapting urban diary ideas to their own approaches, several online examples explicitly recognize the broad applicability of the urban diary tool based on my earlier presentations of the urban diary concept. In Philadelphia, "Philly's Urban Diary" is a work in process that comprehensively approaches "what it means to live in a city" based on a prospective app, a website, public art, audio, video, drawings, comics, and the written word.[64] Another individual is marketing an app called Corner to enhance how particular communities interact in the city and foster human connection.[65]

My urban diary concept has also been cited as the basis for several blogs, class assignments, and journaling pieces.[66] In 2014, Kieu Huynh created a "digital journal" blog entitled *Urban Diary: Small Things to Make a Big Difference*. The blog follows suggestions from my earlier articles on the topic, and contains a variety of subtopics, ranging from "Better City" to "Urban Renewal." Focused on the "feminine city," the effort is notable for its simplicity, and it shows small-scale ideas that are increasingly being implemented by students or otherwise-interested persons looking to communicate how they see the better city.[67]

This chapter has moved from others' conceptions of the city to the critical importance of observing the city firsthand. Following the visual sense through history, we have revisited how we can learn from traditions of immersion and explanation, and from instructive frameworks for seeing. Finally, we have crossed a bridge from the *flâneur* to evolving tools that include the urban diary and web, social media, and smartphone apps.

So far, this book has suggested that better cities might be realized by urban diaries that put observation to work. The urban diary adaptations just mentioned show that some individuals are already implementing urban diary ideas, but basic underlying questions remain. How should we capture the spontaneous human interactions and our relationships with the built environment—inherent in urban diaries—to define and understand our personal cities? What tools should we use? What are the secrets of documenting compelling examples, for ourselves or for sharing with others?

The next two chapters address these questions and provide an in-depth explanation of how to see and document the city through the use of the urban diary tool.

03 SEEING THE CITY THROUGH URBAN DIARIES

—

To photograph is to appropriate the thing being photographed. It means putting oneself into a certain relation with the world that feels like knowledge—and therefore, like power. . . . Photographed images do not seem to be statements about the world so much as pieces of it, miniatures of reality that anyone can make or acquire.

— SUSAN SONTAG
On Photography[1]

The vast range of disciplines at play in urban observation—such as history, planning, architecture, geography, and anthropology—show the richness of inspiration available to us in expressing the city we want. But what we expect of our cities is hardly limited to the vantage points of architects, planners, or social scientists. The common ground for successful places is within each of us, and within the expressions of our senses.

Inspiration often results from historical descriptions of urban change, whether written or visual. From Dickens's writing to the *flâneur*'s legacy, for a very long time observers have been noting the ways that cities evolve. Chronicles of urban change are nothing new; if and when motivated, we can all do our part in providing such accounts every day.

In the visual realm, we have only begun to understand how each of us can adapt and practice tried-and-true photographic techniques

to illustrate our perspectives about urban change. Whether prob-
ing the approaches of historical or modern street photographers,
or users of other camera tools readily available today, we can learn
much about illustration that can be parlayed into what the better city
could be.

This chapter summarizes these traditional approaches and provides
hints about taking better photographs and using them in urban diaries.
I will explain the purposes of an urban diary and conclude with guidance on diary preparation, through a model called the **LENS method**
(**L**ook, **E**xplore, **N**arrate, and **S**ummarize) that readers can adapt as
they see fit. Many practical and inspirational examples also appear
throughout this chapter and chapter 4, as applications of the *Seeing the
Better City* toolkit.

Learning to See and Understand the City

Much of this book is about how to live and record an urban experience,
one with loose (or flexible) rules of observation that allow each of us to
see, think, and then record and respond. The fundamentals of "seeing"
discussed in this chapter show typical diary content and approaches,
and remind us that others, often classified as artists, are well-versed
at using photographs as messaging tools. While this book emphasizes
such photo-driven observation, photos need not be staged or spectacular to send messages to those who influence urban policy and the built
environment.

Perhaps the first modern urban diarist of the sort envisioned in this
book documented the rapid evolution of New York almost 100 years
ago and helped transform the art of urban imagery into a more pragmatic tool of advocacy for how cities should change. Berenice Abbott's
Changing New York showed how photography could chronicle rapid
urban evolution, and it both critiqued and attempted to improve the
planning profession.[2] After returning to New York from Paris, she sys-
tematically photographed New York City with a signature focus on tall
buildings and the changing skyline. In a letter often cited as Abbott's
manifesto on photography and science, she wrote: "We live in a world
made by science. . . . There needs to be a friendly interpreter between
science and the layman. I believe photography can be this spokesman,
as no other form of expression can be."[3] Through her work, Abbott

endorsed those who she believed had a positive influence on the built environment, and she highlighted contrasts between old and new. She hoped urban planners would use her photographs to improve outcomes and support more community-based collaborative planning. She also authored a guide to taking better photos.

In *A Staggering Revolution: A Cultural History of Thirties Photography*, John Raeburn suggests that Abbott's real goal was to display the "unplanning" of New York, based on her strong belief that exposing planning failures should be an obligation of urban photographers.[4] Most importantly, Abbott interpreted the city with multiple layers, as, for example, when she simultaneously saw skyscrapers as both beautiful and ugly, based on application of her nuanced eye:

> I may feel that the skyscrapers are beautiful and majestic. Or I may feel that they are ugly, inhuman, illogical, ridiculous, pathological growths which have no place in the planned city. Whatever I think and feel about the skyscrapers, I say through understanding and application of composition. Vertical lines may seem to topple toward each other, or to fall apart, ready to collapse; they do not create a balanced whole. On the other hand, the photograph may present the skyscrapers in such a manner that verticals sway in a majestic and graceful rhythm expressing unity and order. Even more complex is the problem if the photographer sees the skyscraper as both beautiful and ugly and seeks to create such a duality in the photograph by posing opposite tendencies against each other in dynamic composition.[5]

While urban diaries need not always feature well-composed photographs, they can recreate what political writer Alexander Cockburn once termed "the lost valleys of the imagination."[6] From urban diaries, professionals such as architects, engineers, planners, and lawyers can infer principles of practice based on human-scale dimension addressing the relation between building and street, and associated pedestrian spaces, as well as best practices for lanes, surfacing, and signage. They can allow for what legendary travel photographer Burton Holmes labeled "film as biography" and create a record of an observed time and place.[7]

Figure 3.1   London, England.

Figure 3.2   Buffalo, New York.

Figure 3.3   San Francisco, California.

ACKNOWLEDGING THE SUBJECTIVITY OF SEEING

While this book often celebrates a personal viewpoint, the urban dia-rist may always have to overcome doubts about credibility. Do photo-centric urban diaries risk discredit because of their inherently subjec-tive nature and the convenience of digital editing? I have often heard questions of authenticity raised because images may be manipulated by composition and cropping tools, or through post-processing with appli-cations like Photoshop.

I recall many public hearings where neighbors, sometimes my clients, submitted photo exhibits on the supposed detrimental aspects of a land-use proposal. Sometimes those presentations, even if not post-processed, were subject to criticism for their lack of accuracy or lack of objective scale. Admittedly, it is not difficult to present a proposed new building in a manipulated way, so that it appears to tower over older homes nearby. The risk of that sort of abuse of public process exists regardless, and such practices do not reflect the kind of advocacy I instruct in this book. Rather, urban diaries should be more documentary and inspirational— for instance, using photographs to document existing conditions, to ful-fill the urban diary criteria as set out later in this chapter, or to show exemplary instances of urban development that the diarist finds worthy of emulation in the context of his or her hometown.

While it may be tempting to use angles that purposefully distort, or to use post-processing to create a different story, these efforts do disservice to productive conversation. Instead, aspiring urban diarists should take the time to study the work of accomplished urban photographers like Abbott and her street-photographer forebears, who, as both artists and record-keepers, created undeniably magnetic portraits of urban space and human activity.

Before we return to exploring ways we can make our seeing practical, it is important to dig even further into the subjective side of what and how each of us sees. Designer and bicycle advocate Rob Forbes, in his recent book *See for Yourself* as well as a related 2006 TED Talk, emphasizes this personal element.[8] The guidance that he provides in his own, photographically driven examples—and in the photographs themselves—is foundational in its directness and simplicity. As I do, Forbes champions the camera, which is more "convenient and tolerant . . . than a sketchpad."[9] To some degree, he models his approach on George Nelson's straightforward *How to See: Visual Adventures in a World God Never Made*, a classic photo-rich volume first published in 1977 and republished in 2002 with a new subtitle *A Guide to Reading Our Man-Made Environment*.[10] Nelson believed that few of his contemporaries actually had the skill to read the environment around them, and that education on how to see and rectify deteriorated environments was sorely lacking. He wrote his book as an attempt to cure what he termed "visual illiteracy," a challenge that remains critically important today.[11]

Like Forbes, Nelson wrote not as an urban theorist but as a product designer who gained inspiration from city settings. Both are intuitive about the human condition; Nelson spoke to the virtues of pedestrian space. In his examination of Milan's Galleria and its "levels of meaning"—the multiple social, cultural, locational, and architectural reasons for its long-term resonance—he considered one perspective of return on investment: "Take the great old Galleria in Milan: why would anyone build it? Well, it is right along the big cathedral square. It rains quite a lot in Milan. It also gets very hot in the summer. If you make two streets in the form of a cross, pave the floor with mosaics, fill the building with shops and cafes at ground level, and throw two glass vaults over the streets, pleasant things happen."[12]

Figure 3.4

The Forbes/Nelson approach is eminently humanistic; it empha-sizes individual perception and is centered upon our innate abilities to see. This approach stresses the capabilities within us rather than newer technologies such as the smartphone, apps, neural simulation, and the smart city (also examined in this book). Ironically, however, the very photographic images that Forbes urges us to create are simultaneous "data" for crowd-sourced, aggregated efforts—just as in this book. In other words, in the end, subjective inputs are also the fodder for objec-tive organization, study, and conclusion.

OBSERVABLE BASICS AND URBAN COLOR

Compiling an urban diary often begins with a present focus on a simple thing, whether a sign, a hubcap, or part of a building. Such details of the built environment tap into deeper emotions associated with human feelings and human needs. Seeing becomes a way to marry visceral emotions with the rational world.

According to Forbes, the built environment can be improved through noticing the basics that surround us—for instance, the features of public spaces (do they foster positive or negative emotions?), or inadvertent patterns (is the place "unplanned" in an attractive way, or not?), or the latent power of the color red. The goal is an independent perspective, a point of view, premised on looking and thinking: "If all of us went out on an urban walk with a camera and were asked to take ten photos of anything we found interesting or beautiful, we would see that we all have our own biases and interests. That is a good thing. It accentuates individuality."[13]

The urban diary becomes a platform for practical outcomes by taking these observable basics—such as pattern or color—one more step so "we learn to see and appreciate the common details of our man-made world . . . [and demand] . . . more of our more complex designs and systems, such as our cities."[14] In this context, consider the role of color as an everyday urban experience. No matter that some aspects of color in the city are naturally occurring; manipulation of color is well within the reach of most city dwellers, and is one of the most quickly and affordably altered urban characteristics. The box on page 67 provides examples of specific reference points for urban color, and Urban Diary Excerpt no. 8 on page 68 addresses London diary walks that examine color firsthand in the city. (See also plates 4–16.)

Urban diary entries about observable basics like color can also highlight what architect friends have explained as a growing sustainable-design focus on the end-user experience, rather than the sole pursuit of "green" status through the US Green Building Council's (USGBC) Leadership in Energy and Design (LEED) certifications. Clients now seem to pay more attention to the context and needs of a given project—looking to infuse it with both functional value and some form of positive emotions—and, significantly, the specifics of a building user's interactions with the surrounding urban area. This attention to qualitative aspects of the urban experience is often observable in building

─────────────────────────── HOW COLOR DEFINES THE CITY

C olor is central to how we perceive the urban environment. It is among the first things we notice, and it influences our responses to what we see. The power of color in the city is clear when we feel or when our moods or perceptions change as we view a newly painted building, or as color blends from the unintentional effects of altered light. In sum, then, color . . .

- Distinguishes different features of the natural environment and contrasts them with the built environment.
- Helps define components of the built environment, such as buildings, building features, and structures.
- Distinguishes people from surrounding urban spaces.
- Draws attention to the retail sector through subliminal messaging from vendors and products for sale.
- Emphasizes lettering on public and private signage addressing rules, the location of businesses, and hours of operation.
- Adds interest and attention to rights-of-way (e.g., paths, shared-lane markers), frames safe routes across streets and highways, and regulates different modes of transportation.
- Provides a component of natural or artificial light that brightens the urban night, and fosters safety in darkness.
- Stimulates the urban experience through contrast between built-environment features.
- Is often enhanced by the sun in familiar presentations, particularly sky and water blues, vegetation greens, and building-paint reds.
- Provides dramatic tone and contrast, and can awaken and inspire as part of a local improvement effort.

spaces—such as mid-building or rooftop community areas rich with vegetation and color—and invites associated diary documentation of better city ideals.

Long ago, Berenice Abbott proposed that urban photographers should be mission-based, in pursuit of the better city, consistent with the demonstrative approach she took after her return to New York. Anne Spirn and others have also gone to great lengths to show the potential

---

URBAN DIARY EXCERPT NO. 8

Recently, in London, I found that in walks across a world city, an experience is framed by very simple things. These framing elements include color and light, as well as the ambient sounds of people and place, and a feeling that somehow public and private spaces are interacting seamlessly, safely, and with mutual respect.

Despite the often overcast flat light, London showed a brightness beyond memories of the industrial age. Amid cars and buses and bluster and irregular wear on ornamental facades from long ago, photographs reveal vibrancy and clues of reinvention—exemplified by brighter colors, dynamic new building shapes, bike sharing, classic urban green and safe spaces, and resplendent sidewalk banter and life.

Perhaps it was my imagination or the application of some urban diary technique not present before I learned to look around, but storefronts seemed less like gateways and doors less like barriers, sidewalks more like living rooms and neighborhoods more surrounding of public squares, transit stops, and car-dodging splendor. (See plates 14–16.) In summary, urban diary walks—from Covent Garden to Neal's Yard to Piccadilly to Regent Street, from Hyde Park to Knightsbridge and Chelsea and back—can become movie-like strolls, all about the most famous of urban places becoming new again.

---

for increased use of a visual language in contemplating urban change.[15] So how to go about pursuing these ideals? How to influence the conversation about urban change?

HOW TO PHOTOGRAPH: HELPFUL HINTS

I want to be very careful in suggesting how to practice photography to see the better city. Ansel Adams's simple statements about photography are often cited because they are good reminders that most of us may not need overly technical laundry lists about "how to take good photographs." It is imperative not to prescribe technique. "Mistakes" often lead to stunning results, such as inadvertently missed focus points or accidental exposures, and experimental approaches can create compelling statements about urban life.

Adams's remarks about the role of the photographer are as important as any isolated how-to list. While he stressed "making, rather than simply taking" photographs, he also cautioned that "a good photograph is knowing where to stand" and "there are no rules for good photographs, there are only good photographs."[16] Most importantly, said Adams, "A great photograph is one that fully expresses what one feels, in the deepest sense, about what is being photographed."[17]

Some urban photographers stress the importance of companion storytelling. Others underscore the evocative nature of the photographs themselves. Urban-photography-oriented authors both assemble their words and examples and also provide anthologies of others' examples to show variations in style and approach. Some writers consider topics such as the use of smartphones as stand-ins for conventional cameras, the wi-fi transfer capabilities of both smartphones and the latest digital cameras, and how to use various apps (such as Instagram and Hipstamatic) and online photo-sharing sites to their best advantage.

Fundamentals of preparation, location, photographic gear, and technical elements such as selection of vantage points, lighting, and subject matter are important regardless of the absolute purpose of a photo-centric urban diary. While gear need not be fancy, with the use of smartphone cameras, uploaded imagery, and related apps, it is critical to think about how the variables of technique, composition, and presentation will affect the desired message, and how it may be received.

I have used many readily available resources, coupled with my intuition, to structure my urban diaries discussed here. Introductory guides to photography appear in toolkits that attempt to foster youth and community participation in storytelling with photography. This chapter and chapter 5 adequately describe these approaches. For present purposes, several helpful hints, as assembled by Oregon's Community Health Institute's Participatory Photography Project Guide (and reproduced in endnote 18), are also relevant to any urban diarist.[18] The hints range from simple suggestions about composition, the angle of view, light, lines, patterns, textures, and common mistakes.

A more general book, Henry Carroll's *Read This if You Want to Take Great Photographs*, is another no-nonsense synopsis of photography, readily adaptable to urban diary–making.[19] Carroll focuses on general principles in simple terms, which I believe is most helpful for the urban

Figure 3.5   Never photos without people.

diarist who is not out to become a professional photographer. Carroll uses examples and principles aimed more at becoming comfortable with the process of recording images than the pursuit of perfection.

Along with the guidance summarized here, and the extensive resources also available, I recommend the following approaches to the photography used for urban diaries:

1.   Considering the role of people in photographs is a critical first step. Regardless of the camera, the photographic style, or how-to suggestions, this one, universal parameter applies to any urban photography. Unless the message of the image explicitly relies on empty space, be sure to document surroundings during times that people are using streets and other public spaces, or visibly traveling between private places. Two experienced Seattle council members have driven this point home with interesting stories. Richard Conlin, on the council for fourteen years, described how countless presentations about development projects and other planning and zoning issues focused too much on isolated building cross-sections and elevations, without the necessary acknowledgment of human factors that interplay with new construction.[20] (See plates 17 and 18.)

Similarly, council member Mike O'Brien once wrote to me that the people shown in figure 3.5 on a Seattle sidewalk amid construction provided an element—people—ironically missing from a tour of a new "complete street" earlier the same day.[21] I found the O'Brien comment particularly thought-provoking because of the people-friendly environment intended, but not visually conveyed, by the street redevelopment project.

2. The role of light is elemental. Sometimes it will beautify, but on other days create blandness or overly harsh contrast. While I discourage much manipulation, consider settings that enhance views in the interest of realism, or automatic settings that help in backlit situations. Alternatively, experiment with manual (M), shutter priority (S), and aperture priority (A) settings, or vary exposure using an "exposure compensation" dial to adjust contrast between a bright sky and dark surroundings on the ground.

3. Basic composition is critical, not just to make a good photograph, but to emphasize certain themes that are most relevant to urban diaries. Thematic topics include: illustration of public or private places where people are prone to gather; the edges—hard or soft—between public and private space; transitional features, such as gates, doors, and windows; the spaces between buildings; how transportation modes may overlap or maintain separation; and the edges—also hard or soft—between the natural and built environments. These factors also influence the feeling of safety or threat, which can themselves be fundamental aspects of urban diary.

4. If compiling an urban diary on a daily basis, make multiple visits to profiled locations, and document more than buildings and structures. Consider litter types, wires, antennae, cable dishes, potholes, vegetation (both maintained and unintended), and how they fit into your views of what you like, and what you think should change.

5. In addition to the preceding composition suggestions, consider capturing observations of the contrasts inherent in the city, the juxtapositions discussed in chapter 4, and the tripartite balance of built environment/urban life, people, and nature (man-made green spaces or a leftover natural pocket). This

subject matter is often ripe for governance, as policies, plans and regulations frequently address the many issues associated with balancing competing interests at this intersection of urban development concerns.

6. Pay special attention to the portrayal of height, bulk, and density (the standard terminology for the size and placement of buildings and the number of units on a lot). Here, I suggest more literal interpretation without exploiting angle, distance, zoom, or any post-processing adjustment to alter or distort perception.

7. Do not attempt to sugarcoat a view. Recall that we often need to see the worse city before we argue for the better city. If they are accurate, there is nothing wrong with urban diaries that show socioeconomic problems, poor living conditions, unsafe areas, or infrastructure in need of repair. Often, these "documentary" photographs are the ones that result in action, because of their inherent human stories or because they are shown after tragedies to bring attention to a problem.

8. When using examples from elsewhere to inspire, it is often helpful to compose similar hometown examples. For instance, a Parisian café's approach to open-air seating, facing the street, should be contrasted with a local example. The same would hold true for a Dutch or Danish dedicated bike lane, a Melbourne or Vancouver laneway/alley, or a Lisbon outdoor elevator or tram that serves the Bairro Alto. Are the local versions functional, or mere imitations of a theme? A sensational idea deserves contextual discussions about "fit," with well-documented examples from afar presented paired alongside with a local image. These comparisons demonstrate how local urban assets or dilemmas may be surprisingly universal.

9. Self-criticism is a helpful step. The urban diarist should look carefully at his or her photographs and determine which seem the most successful in communicating any intended messages of endorsement, disapproval, or the encouragement of innovation.

Photographic selection and technique raise a question, discussed later in this chapter and in chapter 4, about whether to preestablish the purpose for any diary journey. Is the urban diary intended as a *dérive-*

URBAN DIARY EXCERPT NO. 9

Traveling in search of emotional bookmarks can become a dangerous pasttime, because romantic interpretations of far-away splendor are smooth and a camera is a willing tool. Many times, I have explored the environs of the Côte d'Azur with an emphasis on the ordinary in order to show the everyday, the mundane, and the lights while walking at night. I have observed the parking lots, read the graffiti, watched the faces, reviewed the signage, experienced life at the post office, and witnessed new development.

Figure 3.6

I always return to Seattle with feelings of renewed inspiration from these ordinary views that suggest a balance of sorts which I've rarely seen elsewhere. As you can see in these photos, the cars of the Côte d'Azur are smaller, the streets narrower, the spaces more multifunctional and human, and nature seems to intermingle more seamlessly. Most of all, the man-made building

Figure 3.7

materials often blend into the sky to create a timeless sense of interaction befitting of the region's long history. It's not all pretty, but there's an organic wisdom at play that escapes words but that photo-centric diaries can capture.

Figure 3.8

like exercise, where the goal is looking itself? Is it simply to record, spontaneously, provocative or interesting observations and juxtapositions? Or is there a more directed reason for preselection of topics, subjects, places, and spaces to photograph?

Is the photo taken with a purpose in mind—to show, for example, a structure or building that is too high, a redevelopment too dense, or disparate from its surroundings? Perhaps snapping the shutter is a response elicited by a request from government or a researcher to share images of, for example, a favorite place? Or, finally, is the project tied to gathering a portfolio in favor of or in response to a particular development proposal, to show harmony, or, conversely, clashes of color or style?

Like those of Adams and Forbes, my diary purpose is often at first subjective (before any consideration of practical use). Many of my photographs comprise emotional markers that I think of as "bookmarks" signaling important human moments—that is, they are observation exercises. These markers are visual examples available not only for personal urban dairies but also for the assembled, crowd-sourced imagery discussed in chapter 5.

How Urban Diaries Draw the City with Light

Photo-centric urban diaries rely on the Greek derivation of the word *photography*—literally, "drawing with light." At its root, a photograph is a frozen moment of the real world, an expression of both eyes and machine, created, as John Berger has noted, with only two raw materials: light and time. It is a drawing or portrayal, which implies creativity; it is also a manipulation of light, but, according to Berger, one that is more like a quotation than anything else.[22] Some consider it evidence, others claim it as art, but, as I've championed throughout this book, photography is my expression of the tangible city, and whenever possible, I use it to inspire urban change by example.

The earliest known "light drawing," or camera photograph (made by Joseph Nicéphore Niépce in 1826 or 1827), is a view out a window at Niépce's estate, Le Gras, in Burgundy, France, showing adjacent buildings and the countryside in the distance.[23] Documenting a personal relationship to surroundings seems a primal tendency, and what better way to communicate this than to depict literally what stands in home-based lines of sight? This integral sort of observation is often the precept of photography workshops for those learning the art (German photographer Julia Baier, for example, requests that her workshop participants first find subjects within 200 meters of home),[24] and helps define subject matter for the photo-centric urban diaries encouraged here. (See plate 19 for Urban Diary Excerpt no. 10.)

Now that we have addressed the fundamentals of how to see, and then how to take better photographs for use in urban diaries, the remainder of this section focuses on my recommended urban diary methodology, the **LENS method** (**L**ook, **E**xplore, **N**arrate, and **S**ummarize), a comprehensive set of diary approaches and parameters. The **LENS** approach uses the basics of seeing described earlier in this chapter, and it structures them around a focus on authentic, individual perceptions ("place-receiving"), our inherent connections to place, our sensitivities to symbols of urban change, and the "urban mirrors" first referenced in chapter 1.

DIARIES ILLUMINATE AUTHENTIC EXPERIENCE

The process of drawing the city with light matured for me during a European trip some years ago, after a long absence. My Paris photograph, depicting people beneath the Eiffel Tower, jump-started my then-dormant fascination with the scenery of urban life and form and the way people use and respond to urban space. The photograph shows the contrast of the Eiffel Tower against the Pont d'Iéna and the Champs de Mars beyond. (See plate 20.)

I intended to record an emotional bookmark with a provocative, dreamlike quality, consistent with my feeling while standing there as I experienced such a beautiful and distinctive urban setting. I used this photograph to illustrate an informal process—"place-receiving"—which emphasizes the response of the actual person in a place. This informal process is the counterpoint to commonly referenced, top-down place-making, and serves as an illustration of the urban diary's value proposition.

Years later, when I compare this photograph to later pictures of Paris and other places, I see many aspirations of visitors, residents, and design professionals, whether realized through spontaneity, tactical approaches, or more applied plans. The photograph suggests several common goals of placemaking, including complete streets, green infrastructure, and other human-scale design methods.

For purposes of experimenting with the meaning of the photo and its implications for placemaking, I have tried five different characterizations. Some are factual and emphasize place names; others seem stale with buzzwords; still others evoke emotion and describe the setting, using the language of climate, color, and the built environment:

- The Eiffel Tower, the Pont d'Iéna, an equestrian statue, cars, buses, and people combine to enhance a Paris view and experience.
- A red bus and red backpack contrast with the Pont d'Iéna, the base of the Eiffel Tower, and the expanse beyond of the Champs de Mars.
- Water and pavement blend in Paris.
- The wet pavement on the Pont d'Iéna actively mirrors people approaching the Eiffel Tower.
- The grainy textures of infrastructure stand out along the Seine.

My summaries could have focused more on the people, or on poetry. The potential variety is open-ended, because place and place-receiving occur as much in our minds—in the soft city—as in the real world. My take from the photograph and my first real attempt at drawing the city with light was a *gestalt* about the many ways to experience a place, and how we should highlight place-users as the most authentic stakeholders of meaning in the urban experience. If we can experience a place with a sense of acceptance and inspiration, then the success of placemaking will be better assured.

City dwellers will benefit from using the tools presented in the **LENS** approach to explore the core relationships of city life and the associated impacts of economic, social, and political decisions on changing urban settings. Urban diaries can play this role through their individual portrayals of the city.[25] Like my Paris photo, urban diaries show us how people use an urban space, and how urban space can be summarized in different ways, depending on perspective.

Photo-centric urban diaries also reveal more if we look at how opportunity expands, as, each day, we move from foot to car, bus or train, and beyond. Documentation of our daily paths suggests a web of movement and associated mutual observation that defines the urban experience. The public realm exists amid and between our respective journeys, on the city's streets, sidewalks, squares, alleys, and parks. In urban diary form, we can discover the embedded patterns—and all of our related, internal and subjective reactions.

Drawing on Allan Jacobs's emphasis on the way inherent clues appear to someone carefully observing urban areas,[26] I suggest that an urban diary might embrace ten observation parameters that help reveal such clues:

1. simple use of color and related aesthetics;
2. incorporation of past uses and economic health of a property or area, whether or not tangible evidence or symbols remain;
3. the role of nature;
4. the relation of building and street;
5. the role of structures other than buildings, such as fencing and furniture;
6. standards for road striping, surfacing, and signage;
7. treatment of corners and setbacks;
8. ways to encourage safe pedestrian spaces for multicultural users of all ages, all while . . .
9. . . . assuring light, air, acceptable noise levels, and . . .
10. . . . appropriate governance of private use of public spaces.

Cultural geographers present a similar catalog of diary-like fundamentals. Christopher Salter's classic approach addresses the city as the primary source: the landscape is the document, and the city is a major chapter. Salter casts human interest in landscape-shaping and landscape-rebuilding as the evidence to be observed, and suggests a methodology for city-reading: "Oh, Say Can You See" (OSAE), where Observation, Speculation, Analysis, and Evaluation guide the observer's journey.[27] In short, observe a landscape element, such as an old corner store, speculate about the reasons for its location, analyze based on follow-up research on the history of the place and, finally, evaluate whether the store still works in its current location. This final evaluation would depend on a variety of factors related to the present and future uses of the surroundings.

DIARIES SHOW HUMAN CONNECTIONS TO PLACE

When counseling clients, or presenting to students, or in book talks, I am often asked how to understand an urban space. In response, I offer five alternative urban diary suggestions for reading and framing surroundings and the way people connect with the places around them:

1. On your next walk from your home to a chosen destination, summarize the experience in one to two paragraphs.
2. Spontaneously visit your five favorite neighborhood locations, and assemble five photographs or short recordings of ambient sounds.
3. Think of a place that you often wish were closer to home. Write about, or photograph, how you would travel from home to there.
4. Videotape a walk, bike trip, or other focused activity along a street.
5. On your camera or smartphone, use a continuous shutter, or "burst" mode to photograph street life that you observe from a passing car, bus, streetcar, or tram.

Depending on the implementation style of the urban diarist, the form and content of the urban diary may change, and so may the way it relays particular connection to place. For instance, the urban diary may be kept in personal notes, or presented as part of an app or upload site like Instagram or Flickr. It might be printed, shown as a Powerpoint or video, or combined with other sense-based compilations addressing sound, touch, or smell. Not every urban diary will be used for advocacy purposes, or as part of a public process or the adjudication of a dispute. It is enough to have an urban diary act only as a prompt to help you look differently at your city and think more about what you see.

Beyond the form of presentation, questions remain about the primary purpose of the urban diary. Is it intended as a learning tool to document existing conditions? Is it an exemplary, inspirational story of comfort and appeal, showing imagery of the better city? Is it actually a catalog of the worse city, filled with examples of conditions to be rectified or conditions resulting from rapid, seemingly out-of-control change?

Plate 1: South Lake Union, night view.

Plate 2: Seattle skyline.

Plates 3: Seattle, Lake Washington viewable factors.

Plate 4: Jerusalem.

Plate 5: Rome.

Plate 6: Nice, France.

Plate 7: Jaffa.

Plate 8: Reykjavík.

Plate 9: Perth, Australia.

Plate 10: Nice, France.

Plate 11: Jerusalem.

Plate 12: Seattle.

Plate 13: Sunbury-on-Thames, England.

Plates 14 and 15: London color.

Plate 16: London color.

Plate 17: People in Fréjus, France.

Plate 18: People in Dublin, Ireland.

Aristotle said that a soul never thinks without a mental image, and perhaps he meant a picture of a city. In that spirit, my 2006 image of Spinola Bay, St. Julian's, Malta, lives on.

The reason is simple. The photograph suggests straightforward and ideal balances as follows:

- A balance of color, dark, and light.
- A balance of people, land, water, and sky.
- A balance of automobiles, boats, and pedestrians commingling.
- A balance of residence, employment, and compactness that seems not only to work but, like a poster, to extol the virtues of urban life;
- An overall inspirational balance of human enagagement and beauty, which is central to discussions about today's cities and to associated "placemaking" initiatives.

This portrait of a former small fishing village literally reflects how the natural features of an island country have now been transformed into a dense urban setting of contemporary dwellings, shops, and restaurants.

Plate 19: Spinola Bay, St. Julian's, Malta.

Plate 20: Paris.

Plate 21: Grasse, France.

Plate 22: Seattle, the concept of juxtapositions.

Plates 23 and 24: Congruity: Budir and Hellnar, Snæfellsnes Peninsula, Iceland.

Plate 25: On a Portuguese railroad bridge adapted to pedestrian and public transit use, an innovative "sidewalk" participant shares the mix-and-match of human and tram. All "streets" need not include all transportation modes.

Plate 26: The backdrop of new development in a historic, scaled riverfront district shows the real change that is well within in the memory of one featured resident along the way.

Plate 27: If water, light, buildings, and people can align so serendipitously, are we missing something magical in the way we discuss and manage urban places?

Plate 28: Street vending gives rise to many of the issues that surround temporary uses of public rights-of-way on streets and sidewalks or abutting private property. What are the rules driven by country, city, or community that address these overlapping "soft edges" of the public and private domain?

Plate 29: When is it environmentally sound, and consistent with human enjoyment and the aesthetic traditions of a French spa town, to densify over water?

Plate 30: Paris, Place de Vosges.

Figure 3.9   A diary prompt.

AN EXPANDED URBAN DIARY

*M*ethods described in chapter 2 suggest how including additional details about urban spaces might enhance interdisciplinary discussion and analysis about an observed physical setting. Here are background ideas, including parameters for initial observation:

1. Observation and reflection on neighborhood public spaces, how and why they exist, the range of activities there, and likes and dislikes of the observer.

2. Examination of the observer's neighborhood on Google Earth, Google Maps, or Google Street View, and what new information these tools provide, as well as what they do not show.

3. Integration with interviews of someone who has lived or worked nearby for many years.

4. Review of media pieces about the observed neighborhood.

5. Review of census data for the census blocks observed, tracking changes such as ethnicity.

6. Location of a prominent place in the area, such as a monument, a public artwork, a museum, a library, a market, or a store, with an explanation of why it matters to the local community.

DIARIES INTERPRET CHANGE IN THE URBAN LANDSCAPE

The urban diary is a kind of archaeology beyond unearthing distinct artifacts from another era—it interprets our urban landscapes, including symbols of change. While urban diaries can be abstract thoughts that exist only in our minds, more tangible recording of our explorations occurs with whatever tool we choose—a pen, a keyboard, or a camera. Any notation about a building, an object, or an underlying relationship shows us actively engaging with a place. Observing this engagement depends on the place-based impacts of four interrelated urban dynamics:

1. The intersection of the built and natural environments;
2. changing modes of transportation, e.g., walking, bicycling, ride share, car2go;
3. the application of associated land-use plans and regulations; and
4. the continuation of or ongoing change to surrounding land uses.

These factors can be observed both as objective elements of the landscape and the built environment and as our subjective responses to the symbols of change that we see. The associated sensations and feelings may be negative or may evoke emotions not always associated with good urbanism, such as fear or sadness. Urban diaries could be used as a way to document conditions, in the spirit of Dickens or Jacob Riis (see his 1890 study of poverty in New York, *How the Other Half Lives*),[28] or, in the manner of a modern *flâneur*, a way to demonstrate the less emphasized elements of urban life.

Consider a diary based on the homeless and where they sleep, whether shop entries, tent cities, parks or other public venues, or on the sidewalk adjacent to vents for discharging heat that emanates from infrastructure below. Such a diary might include some frank encounters with urban locations that are not often glorified, and in fact are often avoided. These types of urban diaries could be compiled at or around noted crime scenes or where tragic events have occurred, or places deemed unsafe where people are told not to go. These places may be as walkable as customary urbanist destinations (such as already-revitalized downtowns or transit-oriented developments), but full of warning and trepidation. Yet, because they often galvanize improvement and reinvention, they may be the best motivation for urban diaries that ultimately seek vitality, safety, and a sense of predictable order.

On the other hand, urban diaries often feature points of beauty that may be much-photographed focal points over time; urban aesthetics remain a classic attribute of the better city, as noted by Abbott (see chapter 2). In Seattle, as a predicate to the establishment of the Olmsted park system, John C. Olmsted and his assistant, Percy Jones, photographed key views, topography, indigenous plants and other urban development characteristics as part of the "intelligence phase" of Seattle park planning.[29] This can be further realized in the urban context through traditional photographs of "beautiful" city settings, including postcard views and particularly evocative night scenes.[30]

DIARIES REFLECT URBAN MIRRORS AND TEACHING MOMENTS

One of the most compelling aspects of an urban diary (also championed by some of the traditional urban observation approaches summarized in chapter 2) is finding vantage points in the city where people watch people—essentially, small-scale human observatories amid the dynamic urban landscape. From such places, we can sit on the edge of, or within, public places and discern the goings-on reflected by the so-called urban mirrors referenced in chapter 1. Using these casual observation points, we can observe human conduct alongside the built environment.

Urban mirrors are often found in safer spaces in the public realm, such as active streets, corners, and squares. Places that lend themselves to being urban mirrors are more common in cultures where neighbors readily interact, and where the boundaries between public and private life blur. From these vantage points, spontaneous "teaching moments" inspire us in a "look at that!" sort of way.

These "teaching moments" show how urban spaces change when we observe others as participants in our experience. While looking at urban gathering places, I usually have my eyes open for sudden, unique (and often private) moments in public spaces—moments that can serve as inspiration for policies and designs that encourage authentic human behaviors.

In Grasse, France—the subject of earlier photos—I recently saw just such a teaching moment, no doubt part of a special mother/daughter excursion to the famed Grasse *parfumeries*. Here, with the benefit of late

Figure 3.10   An urban mirror.

afternoon sunlight, long shadows, and shaded background, I was able
to capture colorful matching attire that blended with daily urban life.
This urban diary moment presented an uncontrived spirit and sense of
place that felt particularly remarkable. (See plate 21.) I was fortunate to
snap the photo from an "urban mirror" position on a small pedestrian
street branching off from a central square. This vantage point allowed
me to record interactions on a small public stage. Often, these urban
diary opportunities are obvious to the beholder, and it's essential to
record their locations for later reference and discussion because they
show us people at their best within compelling urban spaces.

How to Prepare an Urban Diary

The urban diary reflects and assembles our urban mirror observations, including the intersection of the public and private realms, the boundaries of the built and natural environments, the relationships between land uses and transportation, and issues of adaptive reuse and public safety.

Determining the importance and significance of particular starting points and pathways is a good first step (as examined further in chapter 4). Possibilities for pathways range from a functional outline of home–work activity, a document of urban change, or a *dérive*-like interaction between personal/internal cities, showing underlying overlaps, juxtapositions, hints of history, or sources of happiness, sorrow, or fear. In any event, the power of the image itself may make detailed description unnecessary as the picture may be "worth a thousand words." Or, it may not be that its meaning or underlying personal significance becomes apparent until the photo appears on the screen, adjacent to other photographs.

As chapter 4 further explains, this process sounds linear, but it need not be, as the Situationists (see chapter 2) have reminded us by urging us to "drift." The internet is bloated by essays (including some of my own) of linear travels up straight streets, with sequential photographs emulating the flip-decks of old. But our personal cities are not so simple. There are multiple points of entry and ways of experiencing place that at first disorient rather than orient, and then may invoke a search for order.[31] These experiences can be recorded as well in order to contrast with rational, objective approaches to approving or allowing change, such as the land-use regulatory-approval process.

Urban diaries also inevitably raise issues of where and how land-use regulation should take place. For instance, how should a government decide where uses should mix rather than remain separate, or where to allow more flexibility in building height? A focused, diary-like approach by city planning staffs might enhance or redefine methods of accomplishing sensible change.

In one example, a planner friend in an Australian city has related how a developer once questioned why the land he owned had been left outside of an urban-renewal area, one block adjacent, that would have allowed him to build to eight stories in height rather than four. His property was in a designated "no change" area under a newly approved plan. The planner and her supervisor, who both arrived in the city after the delineation of this boundary, wandered around the renewal area as if performing a Situationist "drift," recording their impressions with a camera. Notably, they followed this urban diary approach *after* the designation of "no change" occurred. Consequently, my friend understood the value that would have been realized by a photo-based public input effort early in the urban-renewal process.

Her retroactive suggestions to the city zoning authorities included asking interested parties to wander the area to determine hard and fuzzy boundaries, identifying areas with perceived capacity to change and areas better left untouched. She also found early input lacking on how the city's renewal delineations would affect the streetscapes (including permitted building forms, access to sunlight and shadow avoidance, and historic preservation issues). Her story influenced the design of the **LENS method** (**L**ook, **E**xplore, **N**arrate, and **S**ummarize) and its urban diary approaches and parameters that follow, below.

A SUMMARY OF THE URBAN DIARY METHODOLOGY: LENS

The **LENS method** (**L**ook, **E**xplore, **N**arrate, and **S**ummarize) is a comprehensive set of prospective diary approaches and parameters. The urban diarist will rarely select all parameters listed here, since the use of particular parameters will depend on purpose and location. (Chapter 4 contains further applications of **LENS** features.)

First, pick your *tool*. Mine is a camera and still photography. The camera can be your smartphone camera, and you can use video rather than static images. Or you can write, record audio, tweet, use Facebook entries, Instagram posts, Flickr uploads, or compile some or all of these in a blog.

Traditionally, my **LENS**-style urban diaries have been typological or theme-based, centered on one or more of the following:

- Corner/Intersectional
- Walkable
- Modal Pathway—walk / bike transit
- Street feature (e.g., woonerf)
- Sit-able

- Juxtapositional (see chapter 4)
- Stratigraphical/Historical/Age Value (see chapter 4)
- Shareable
- Homeless (tents, under overpasses, parks, doorways, tent cities, worse city)
- Appian Entry (see chapter 4)
- Squares
- Spaces between
- Interior spaces
- Delightful/Children in squares

With these general guidelines and the examples throughout this book in mind, it is time to try your hand at compiling your urban diary, and to use your senses to assess the city you *have* as opposed to the city you *want*.

First, choose your **urban diary type**, e.g., orientation, Via Appia method (see chapter 4) as introductory walk? Or perhaps *Flâneur*, Journal, Social Comment, Travel Guide, Wayfinder, Public Comment (in favor of or opposed to a particular plan/project), Architectural Criticism, Photo Essay, Sketchbook, or Comparative Analysis.

Next, pick a **starting point**. What is your location?

Now, attempt to obtain a **pre-diary overview** from Google Maps or Google Street View. The use of these tools is for orientation only and should not substitute for the on-site investigation itself.

Pick your **mode of travel**, and decide whether you intend a linear path, or a drift, or even an attempt to get lost. Do you wish to adopt the Flaneur Society's purposeful approach to getting lost? Consider how your sensations will change if you are walking, biking, or driving, and whether you are the driver or passenger. The ideal, of course, is to walk, to assure maximum sensation.

Establish some **initial goals** for your investigation. Examples include: Simple orientation; getting to know a new city or neighborhood; creating a "desire map"[32] and undertaking an associated journey around acquiring a needed good or service; assessing how to improve your home–work commute; determining forms of urban development that you do or don't like; better understanding the human–urban interface and how people change the city (such as through spontaneous small-scale rebuilds); exploring urban expression (graffiti, sandwich boards, signage); developing comments for public process; making a comparison with things you like from another neighborhood or city.

Choose your LENS parameters. Your observed parameters may change according to your goals, but reserve the ability to adopt a *dérive* approach and free-form, riff-and-follow sensations. Assess types of photos or focal points for other diary tools and implementation techniques. Here's what I have found to be inherently the most revealing, given the observation parameters outlined above:

Overview

- Keystone, overview observations—for example, a linear street portrait, a bird's-eye view from a hill or tall building, where possible, or a skyline view.

People–Place Focus

- People–place interactions wherever relevant: illustrations of relationships with surroundings, activities, and, where available, identities of people portrayed.
- Will you search for crowds and associated opportunities to mingle with those assembled?

Diary Subject Matter and Inquiry

Will you seek out public spaces such as parks, squares, dedicated building spaces, and markets? How will you move within and around them?

- Role of transportation modes.
- Role of nature, generally.
- Role of light and color, generally.
- Role of history: symbols, "ghosts," building stratigraphy, monuments. What is traditional, inherent?
- Role of change: observations of identifiable change in the urban landscape.
- Notation of how places survive differently.
- Where public/private spaces meet or overlap: convergence points (corners), adequacy of sidewalk frontage space, juxtapositions/incorporations of old/new, nature/built, color, enhancement of dense residential frontages (doors, windows, balconies).

- Role of height and scale: observations of compatibility or lack thereof under existing conditions or new construction; compromise to the presence of nature and light.
- Identify known juxtapositions.
- Accessory features: street furniture to accommodate human needs (shelter, sitting, watching, privacy), fences, hedges (safety).
- Spontaneity and everyday urbanism (graffiti, unregulated signage, temporary or pop-up uses, unintended uses).

Governmental Specifics

- Safety parameters: crime prevention through environmental design (CPTED): barriers, lighting, eyes on the street, mode separation that allow for seamless contextual traditions between different transit modes.
- Role of known government intervention in permitting, or enforcing. Does it help/hinder your experience?

Finally, identify a **provisional end point**, and then begin your urban diary journey and investigation, using the documentation approaches and examples contained in chapter 4 and the urban diary excerpts presented throughout the book. By doing so, you will marshal the many parameters discussed so far—such as color, light, nature, structure, history, and juxtapositions—into a distinctly personal approach to seeing the better city.

When you've completed your urban diary walk, consider **conclusions and use.** Assemble photographs in a way that can be presented to inspire and show what is possible, in context—what might be adaptable, what not. Show people in the context of a particular urban space. An urban diary should address human character through the senses of the urban diarist, which may not always dictate a quest for "good" or "harmonious" architecture, urban planning, or design. Disorder or surprise may be as much a part of one person's better city as another's focus on scaled buildings and consistency. Organically evolved spaces and places that show their age and historical context may be more pleasing than the imposition of something new.

As explained in previous chapters, one critical role of an urban diary is to help the diarist determine which alternative might resonate for his or her personal city. Why do announced plans for a neighborhood seem inappropriate? Why does a proposal for a property's redevelopment seem not to fit? To participate in a discussion that answers these questions, we should understand the root causes of human visual response and the fundamentals of how pieces of the visual environment contribute to the whole.

The next chapter takes the background learning and loose structure of the **LENS** method from this chapter and will continue to address these questions and explain how to capture common-sense portraits of our personal cities, and why.

04 DOCUMENTING OUR PERSONAL CITIES

—

What strange phenomena we find in a great city, all we need do is stroll about with our eyes open. Life swarms with innocent monsters.

– CHARLES BAUDELAIRE
"Miss Scalpel"[1]

An urban diary journey to, or through, a site or a space need not present a built environment that is symmetrical or otherwise extraordinary, nor must it feel modern or pristine. One point of the urban diary is to illuminate whether a space succeeds in a local context, as a balanced place of comfort and scale. This, of course, depends on who is looking.

While chapter 3 described the nuts and bolts of putting together a photo-centric urban diary, this chapter shifts to "advanced topics": how to think about urban observation, particularly through photography, as a kind of visual archaeology, recording the successes and failures of present-day urban settings for both clues about the past and ideas about how to shape the future. Although use of the word *diary* clearly indicates the personal element of this observation approach, the components of creating an urban diary described in this chapter—following pathways, identifying juxtapositions, homing in on small, interesting details, and more—offer the diarist a way to emphasize viewpoint and express the unique appeal of a place (or not).

Basic urban design principles are helpful references, as well as the approaches to observation discussed in chapter 2. Urban-design scholar and textbook author Matthew Carmona and colleagues summarize the visual characteristics of urban spaces, and they note naturalness (natural over built features), upkeep, blending of open and defined space, historical significance, and order ("coherence, congruity, legibility, clarity") as factors that help explain the human preference for a thriving place.[2]

Carmona also underscores philosopher and critic Walter Benjamin's unconscious perceptions (see chapter 2), and the role of *gestalt* principles such as similarity, proximity, common ground / common enclosure, orientation, overall enclosure, and continuity. Finally, Carmona stresses the role of pattern, balance, rhythm, and harmony in the way that new additions may relate to an overall urban space.[3]

If a portion of an urban diary involves taking and assembling photographs as set out in chapter 3, the factors listed by Carmona should provide navigational hints but should not dictate results. The following built-environment elements all play a part in creating urban spaces: buildings, structures, paved and unpaved streets and sidewalks, varied forms of natural and constructed landscaping, benches, signs, covered spaces, and lighting. Areas that succeed in attracting people will likely supply a recordable, visual mixture that is appropriate and is in context, a mix that the urban diarist can perceive and summarize as supportive of a tangible sense of place.

In counseling how best to capture personal cities through urban diaries, I follow the orientation of "urbanism without effort" toward urban fundamentals that ultimately define our physical surroundings. When stuck, when feeling defeated in understanding or in expressing what all of the complexities of the city might mean, I return to the first principles of urbanism referenced in chapter 1. *All helpful hints about exploration and observation in the urban setting inevitably relate to the human needs that define urban space and place, and the emotions that surround them.* It follows that we should be vigilant about the basic human needs, routines, patterns, and responses that we all share, from some form of shelter, a place to work or a means to survive, and the transportation from shelter to work, where we intersect with the cities around us.

We can use simple self-prompts like "I am hungry," "I am lonely and need to share," "I need milk at the store," "I want to get to work early today," "I want to read a book," or "I need to go for a run." By doing so, we find our versions of the elementary journalistic "who, what, when, where, why, and how." This self-awareness will further define our paths, our modes of transportation, who we will see, how we will be affected by the weather and other factors, and how we feel about the residential, commercial, public, or institutional spaces of the city. It is through these fundamental pathways, destinations, and associated sense-based experiences that we create our urban diaries.

As for myself, whenever I have a camera I document these small, urban adventures as they play out. I decide, after observing with the assistance of photographs, what is better or worse, and I begin the brainstorming process on how to improve what I see. For those who wish to indulge other senses, maybe the diary is about smells or temperature, or the music that they hear. Earlier chapters provided several perspectives on this subjective city and its importance. Our personal, individual cities can emerge from purposeful observation undertaken reflectively by each of us, and not only from responding to someone else's often manipulative point of view. This chapter moves beyond photographic technique into ways of eliciting our personal cities and expressing their elements for practical use.

When a Neighborhood Walk Is More than a Stroll

Although many of my urban diaries originate with inspirational observations overseas, many also come from everyday notation of the attributes of the area where I live, Seattle's Madrona neighborhood. Madrona is one of Seattle's oldest neighborhoods, and it slopes down toward Lake Washington with sometimes dramatic views that benefit from an Olmsted-designed park system first implemented over 100 years ago. This historical setting offers remnants and stories that reflect the sociocultural evolution of the city (such as lender "redlining" practices that once precluded loans to minorities).

The Madrona palette, therefore, is well suited for looking around, noticing, and memorializing a personal city in diary form. This opportunity for camera use is not surprising; as noted in chapter 3, when John C. Olmsted first traveled to Seattle in 1903 to commence his firm's park-planning work, he and his assistant observed the city landscape, vantage points, and potential park properties with a camera.[4]

I conceptualized the urban diary idea after years of photography-based walks in Madrona, even noting in an early blog piece, detailed below, that a morning walk was a fine excuse for actually creating places with the attributes I saw while strolling by.

On these walks, often over the same routes on different days, I noted things like the low-rise, eclectic, and mixed-use spirit of commercial buildings adjacent to residences. I saw a particularly busy corner where a building's frontage features a diagonal entryway instead of perpen-

Figure 4.1

dicular walls, which creates a bridged seating and activity space across the street from a public playfield (see fig. 4-1). I learned how traditional neighborhood uses evolved from historical, neighborhood-oriented uses to boutique small businesses and restaurants. I photographed and wrote about sandwich-board advertising for these businesses, and about shareable uses such as an ice cream shop merged with a laundromat.

I documented many other neighborhood features, such as stairways cutting through steep hills to assure lake access (see fig. 4-8) and alleys that fostered neighbor-initiated alley movie nights. Nearby, I saw pocket parks left over from land donations from long ago, eclectic sewer grates, remnant cobblestone or red-brick streets or street sections, dramatic water/mountain views, and sidewalks disrupted by large tree roots. Once, on a dog walk, I encountered, and later wrote about, a sidewalk-sharing coyote that emerged from Madrona Woods (areas of which have been recently restored by work groups from the neighborhood).

Sometimes my photographs have been delightfully redundant in showing what similar neighborhood icons, such as a painted brick sign, looks like with different cameras, by both day and night. I have taken many photographs of the same signs (including "notice of proposed land-use action" signs signifying change, political and real estate

Figure 4.2

signs, and commercial sandwich boards advertising neighborhood businesses), the same benches, the same views over Lake Washington, and
various places where sidewalks flare out and people can gather. Not to
mention the Adirondack chairs outside the coffee shop (see fig. 4-1), the
odd piece of infrastructure composed of pipes and meters (that seems
to keep growing), the buses, the neighborhood grocery, and the multi-
family dwellings made to look like single-family homes. Along with the
changing people in the barber shops and stores, and pets on the streets,
the urban fabric motivated me to no end, and exploring and observing simple neighborhood blocks like mine is an accessible pastime for
anyone.

   In more recent years, Madrona has been a stage set for examples of
the densifying city, with contrasts of transportation modes, new mixed-
use projects, and associated architecture more apparent lately than in
recessionary years. Capturing, processing, and sharing responses to this
kind of change became the drivers for this book. Regular photography shows a variety of building styles built within the zoning envelope, but also ongoing changes to the nature and mix of uses along the

Figure 4.3 Changing Madrona

neighborhood's commercial street. Over time, restaurants, live–work buildings, and other mixed-use buildings have proliferated further. Then sidewalks have improved, and changed shape. Simultaneously, older conventional houses have disappeared and the streetscape collectively has altered its color and, some would say, its character as well.

While Madrona may have provided me with inspiration, it is just one example of places worth observing that can be found and compared to venues elsewhere; in my case, in Seattle, I have observed and chronicled the evolution of urban form mostly seeded in a young city whose primary features crystallized just as the automobile was maturing in the United States. But no matter where we reside, what we can see can be read and compared, and can provide aspirational examples or lessons to be avoided. I cannot repeat enough the importance of patient immersion and the ability to generate these ideas from within.

I have learned a great lesson in taking equivalent diary walks across the world that set the stage for acknowledging the human universals so central to my writing, and these lessons are interspersed throughout this book in words and images. "That reminds me of . . ." has become a powerful phrase—and another major motivation for this book.

For instance, in the subtle curve of a red Madrona apartment building with first-floor retail (which I seem to photograph with obsessive repetition), I am transported to old mixed-use areas of Glasgow, Scotland, or commercial areas next to the Old Town in Edinburgh. Similarly,

Figure 4.4

in Seattle's Greenwood neighborhood, former mayor Mike McGinn showed me how a pub business in Greenwood had transformed a wall to a half-wall in order to facilitate semi-private community outdoor space blending with the street. I remembered walk-by spaces in several other places and recalled similar outdoor seating areas on Lisbon's Alfama hill, where the human scale and interaction between private and public realms were second nature to local residents.

As already noted, urban diaries and their look-see-and-process mindset were how I first identified with the popular "placemaking" term. During the recent recession, I would frequently stroll with expenditure-sensitive "quick fixes" in mind, in order to generate comparisons between places I had seen around the world, and I would focus on how different cultures address similar human needs or typical urban

Figure 4.5

Figure 4.6

conditions. To some degree, the images that I created speak for themselves, but I believe it is important to nudge the reader in order to assure that the communication is successful. In one instance, in the list below, I addressed the prospect of enhanced street life and the need for perceived safety among prospective street users, and I asked how Seattle might achieve the successes of narrow European streets and of laneways in Melbourne, Australia. Photographs—and the *de facto* urban diary—defined the following "first steps," in the hope of easy wins, consistent with multiple public dialogues about the enhancement of alleys, public spaces, street appearance, and safety:

1. Emphasize an alluring focal point.
2. Emphasize vines, branches, hanging flowers, and plants.
3. Use simple, green plantings and encourage ornamental building features in the path of view.
4. Where possible, enhance multi-level exposure to vernacular buildings amid the urban fabric.
5. Provide varied forms of encounter with surrounding commercial uses.
6. Celebrate exotic signage.
7. Provide for a multicolor, mixed-use environment.
8. Simultaneously amplify angle, color, and texture to highlight organic street life.
9. Enhance structural features to frame places en route.
10. Celebrate the marketplaces of vending and dining.
11. Make angles magical.
12. Highlight iconic buildings.

In another urban diary referenced above, I explained how simple neighborhood walks can further show the predicament and challenge of adapting public and private to the old and new, and I suggested some additional "quick wins." I suggested the following "starter principles" for ongoing consideration, all in association with photographic illustrations:

1. Don't forget the school building and surroundings, even in trying times. School districts may have limited funds, but coalesce around parent-driven nonprofit organizations to keep the focus on the neighborhood school.

Figure 4.7   Laneway inspiration.

2. Initial American attempts at outdoor commerce can be mono-
    chromatic. Businesses that give rise to street life should be
    encouraged, both through flexibility in public permitting
    (and the assessment of street-use fees) and also private encour-
    agement to add color and appeal.
3. Scooters are becoming increasingly visible. We need to know
    the rules for parking, and enforcement of these rules needs
    to allow for "overburdening" striped or customary vehicle
    spaces.

4. Often, interim bike striping is the only affordable means for a city to encourage the use of bicycles and simultaneous use of streets with other transportation modes. Rules of the road are not enough to assure safety. At a minimum, work with advocacy groups to monitor repainting needs and visibility, and work with preexisting business to integrate with necessary and historic ingress and egress.

5. Reuse, integration, mode splits, diversity of paving, walkable paths, and mixed housing types are often already a part of cities, predating the widespread application of American zoning in the 1920s. Learn from, adapt, and integrate what is already there.

6. Finally, pedestrians walk with pets. Public and private approaches to pet tie-up locations should not be forgotten.

Figure 4.8

With waterfront redevelopment in mind, I compiled other comparative photographs to show how shore-side venues once reliant on marine commerce now feature retrofits adapted to the needs of modern housing, transportation, and tourism. I used pictures to show how, in the ideal urban setting, waterside venues are optimal places of human interaction and are often destinations on longer treks across neighborhoods and particularly symbolic of the politics of placemaking: who gets and who pays amid the unfolding challenge of how to fund and maintain public space.[5]

I used the photographs to suggest six elements of the "walkable waterside," with the goal of inspiring a private role in public placemaking for amenities otherwise financed through public tax dollars, bond issues, levies and the traditional suite of urban revenue generation:

1. Walking places.
2. Biking places, with enabled separation from other transportation modes.
3. Places of congregation, recreation, and observation.
4. Intermingling of water-dependent trades.
5. Food along the way.
6. Natural settings blended with the urban fabric.[6]

The Role of Personal Emotion

For some, documenting personal cities is as simple as the ready use of a smartphone and social media sharing of one or more photographs to document daily urban life, often with lighthearted provocation and commentary. I am frequently guilty of filling my Facebook page or Instagram uploads with quirky pictures that show something humorous about my neighborhood, my hometown, or a city faraway. Often, these photographs show signs that have unintended or amusing messages, red cones in the street adopting human characteristics, multicolored trash and recycling receptacles in odd configurations, custom tree ornaments that seem to clash with design requirements, attempted control of transportation modes gone awry, and other curious or random juxtapositions. Other, more serious examples include documenting potholes, showing land-use application notices, and tracking various stages of new construction.

Figure 4.9   Lighthearted display of bottles.

I have seen others do the same, often on regular walks or in daily postings, with wry comments about urban policies or uncontrolled growth. Clearly some have an agenda, often "concern trolling" or indirect communication to politicians. Others post photos—most often during election cycles—to support or oppose political candidates' plans.

While these sorts of limited photo essays may not be full-blown urban diaries of the sort contemplated here, I often see one practical result. Even if met with little more than a designated Facebook "like" or a short, humorous comment (some public figures, political candidates, or media personalities generate hundreds of comments per photo), they spur reflection and, occasionally, follow-up conversation. Even without the purposeful use of a conventional camera, these mostly smartphone-generated pictures have a documentary purpose and, most importantly, they allow us to exercise and share our fundamental immersion and experiential skills.

For other people, personal cities and emotions about where we live sometimes depend on more poignant events faraway, especially those that occur in iconic, international urban places central to the interpretation of city life and urbanism. Recent terrorist incidents in Paris, Brussels, Nice, Istanbul, and other cities have reinforced universal concerns about safety and security in our urban areas, and, in a time of countless other instances of gun violence, we often express fear of similar events occurring in our daily lives. In particular, twice during 2015, images of chaos in Paris were superimposed over the idyllic views of urbanism.

My misty night photographs of Paris from 2014 took on new meaning as depicting more innocent urban scenes: the outdoor restaurants in the Parisian night, the gatherings of people of all sorts in markets and stores amid coffee, monuments, books, and more, whether inside or outside usual tourist venues. I saw in my photographs those smiles uniquely characteristic of twilight emotions in the city that is perhaps our greatest example of the merger of people and place. By the time of my return to Paris in February 2016, the social-interaction elements of earlier photos were still there, but it was now difficult (and likely illegal) to photograph the increased police and military presence (including military patrols) around certain landmarks and religious structures, and in certain *arrondissements*.

Many people's Parisian urban diaries typically include portrayals of the better city—an archetype of urban landscapes that personifies the nuanced charm first captured by epic street photography. But those landscapes were, for all practical purposes, assaulted in November 2015. In place of symbolic Parisian imagery were overturned chairs, bodies on the ground, and faces reflecting tragedy. Certainly this is the "worse" city—our greatest fears, noted in chapter 1 as perhaps a necessary prequel to finding the better counterpart. Whether a simple social media post or a more involved urban diary entry, photography captures the full range of the human emotions connected to a place.

Urban Diaries Away from Home

In post-2015 Paris, the emotional reclaiming process is part of the inevitable urban dynamic and our human capacity to rebuild. Often this dynamic, when on display, shows uniting rather than divisive themes in

Figure 4.10   The reclaimed Place du République.

the urban landscape. Visiting and photographing cities can stress these positive dynamics, and can inspire rebuilding and healing processes as needed.

In these instances, qualitative and interactive experiences, along with comparison, seem more important than assembling smart city-data points. The qualitative and experiential also adds necessary personal dimensions to media representations of cities undergoing change or facing urban-planning challenges. For instance, actually visiting a place you have read or heard about—such as the changing face of East London—provides a firsthand reference for comparison with the impact of similar "gentrification" back home.

Another facet of photographing away from home comes from that indescribable human dance of history, people, and place that occurs when, while traveling, we simply like what we see. It is exciting when something resonates and invites a photograph—perhaps a special urban space, or a building, or a fragment of what was, preserved either purposefully or inadvertently. Sometimes these experiences produce a simple, irrational *gestalt*: a sudden wish to live in the vacation venue for a year rather than a day . . . or at least to take the places home.

As an example, in *Urbanism Without Effort* I wrote about the Cinque Terre in northwest Italy, five towns now preserved as "artifacts" in a designated World Heritage Site, connected by footpath, rail, and water. Their magically photogenic amenities of street, square, and housing are, in reality, far more than facade-based touristic shells, dominated in the summer by strangers rejoicing in local wine and pesto, the absence of cars, and the wonders of a small-scale, interurban trek. As photocentric urban diary subjects, the towns' inspirational "we like what we see" elements—walkability, vibrant color, active waterfronts, and seamless interface with terraced landscapes— allow us to import the gift of urban ideas for potential implementation.

An excited emotional response to an urban place while traveling does not always require an overseas journey to a place like the inspirational footpaths between the Cinque Terre towns. Recently, I was highly motivated to photograph the revitalization of downtown Detroit, now proceeding rapidly. On a visit to San Francisco in 2011, during a walk from the Financial District to Telegraph Hill, I encountered a series of urban diary scenes so evocative that they seemed at first staged for the camera. These views emphasized people, bright color, and active settings; in contrast to the "worse city" views of terrorist incidents, they show the positive and dynamic side of urban perception and the full range of emotions away from home.

Figure 4.11   San Francisco dynamic theme: Urbanity on display.

URBAN DOCUMENTATION CONSIDERATIONS AWAY FROM HOME

Generally, consider the following when compiling an urban diary while traveling:

1. If you are traveling to a place with a venerable urban history, be on the lookout for inspirational examples that, if applied in context, might improve an urban space at home. For instance, the idea for New York's High Line came first from Paris.

2. Beware of nostalgia when observing historic landmarks and places. It is not surprising to be motivated or awestruck; the challenge is to think about why. What is it about seeing such a place, or otherwise sensing it, that causes any particular reaction?

3. Use a camera shutter as a reflexive tool. Snap when feelings dictate a sensation; composition need not always be the initial goal.

4. Consider annotating why something seems significant in a text or voice note. This is very important when traveling, as it may not be easily possible to retrace steps or return to a place that seems significant in order to verify details about the location or the circumstances of a given photo.

5. Guidebooks are helpful, but linear or literal travel is not necessarily the most authentic experience. Recall the role of the *dérive* and Situationist interpretation. If it's safe, follow curiosity—sights and smells. On the other hand, be mindful. I once followed graffiti through narrow passages in Jerusalem's Old City and ended up in a courtyard, surrounded by a group of men. Even though the courtyard was "public," I was promptly asked to leave.

6. If traveling outside your home country, consider how juxtapositions seem different. Private and public space, pavement surfaces, natural and built, transportation modes, eras of construction on infrastructure and buildings, to name but a few, all may overlap in unaccustomed ways. It is often worthwhile to ponder why.

7. Looking at redevelopment projects reveals good focal points, as these projects tend to be emblematic of change, yet can seamlessly blend with existing conditions. Reinvented urban

space need not be controversial for failure to honor existing fabric and context. Track responses carefully. In Nice, France, I am constantly aware of the blended interplay among pedestrians, buses, automobiles, and trams downtown in the post-tramway era, without the need for signage or traffic direction.

8. Follow basic human needs as starting urban diary themes. They will define what you see along the way. They may be as simple as the characteristics of where people live, or where the less fortunate find a place to sleep, or the locations available for a trip to a store, restaurant, or café. Depending on distance, these factors will likely influence the chosen mode of transportation and the way crossings occur with other people's paths. At home, similar choices may create journeys (and diaries) that look entirely different.

9. Center on people and, as already noted, attempt to include them in photographs, even from afar. How we see people interacting with the physical environment, in combination with other factors, will influence what we take away from exploration and observation.

10. Consider how light guides perception. Depending on climate and color, an urban diary may assume a different mood.

Figure 4.12   Modal interplay in Nice.

Figure 4.13   Center on people.

11. Emphasize the role of scale of the built environment and its appeal for street life. Many have written about the way that areas with diverse commercial street life and windows open to view (or other forms of soft edges) will create a different response than blank walls or other forms of limited accessibility.

Following a Pathway

Whether I am exploring in my neighborhood or traveling elsewhere, I am constantly aware of the efficiency of the linear arterial versus the possibility of wandering, or straying from the most direct path in the spirit of the Situationist *dérive*. Route choices, even if circuitous, require attention, because any choice of path may hold clues about observed features and associated personal reactions to urban space. As explained in chapter 3, urban diary approaches should not be prescriptive, yet after many years of observing cities around the world, I have increasingly noted some preferred exploration patterns, including an emphasis on a pathway approach to noticing the city.

VIA APPIA, ROME, ITALY: "CLASSICAL ENTRY"

Entering a city or neighborhood along a classical pathway is often the best way to experience urban space and the most suitable for urban diary use. In some parts of the world, former hunting or shepherds' paths have evolved into streets and highways. In other cases, military roads have become major thoroughfares fulfilling an entryway purpose significantly different from what was originally intended.

Consistent with the psychogeography and "ghost" encounters discussed in chapter 2, I believe that the rediscovery of underlying elements along urban pathways is of analytical value to the urban diarist and informative about how to make a better place. While traveling the pathway, we can usually see the evolution of uses, styles of architecture, and transportation challenges from which to learn and understand some of the negative feelings we may experience as we pass through a place. Once the diarist is aware of the potential for this sort of "visual archaeology," the urban diary shows context clues.

My favorite pathway story illustrates visual archaeology at its best: the experience of entering a modern city, surrounded by thousands of

Figure 4.14

years of artifacts—of differing scales—that come into view as the journey proceeds. It includes an intentional method of walking into Rome on the historic Via Appia, which grants the perspective of a soldier reentering the city by military road—without any need for a virtual reality device. Along the walk, it is possible to see the stratigraphy of the city firsthand and note the overlay of one era upon another. The process involves taking a train to the outskirts of the modern city, taking a short walk to find the Via Appia within the regional park system, and following the road—with original paving stones—back into Rome. On this walk, the urban diarist sees history unfold in a real-time way, beginning with serial views of the ancient roadside tombs of the wealthy, continuing with passage through medieval and Renaissance city gates, and culminating with the entry walk through the landmark Arch of Constantine.

The Via Appia entry walk explains multiple histories of Rome and the "age value" of different development eras. Similar experiences occur on circumnavigational walks around walled cities elsewhere in Europe (such as Lucca, Italy), or when viewing the integration of structural remnants with later buildings (such as Diocletian's Palace in Split, Croatia). In a more modern application, the form of Seattle's Capitol Hill neighborhood is readily explained by the leftover auto showrooms that are now part of facade-preservation efforts within the boundaries of the area's Pike/Pine Overlay District.

ROYAL MILE, EDINBURGH, SCOTLAND: PATHWAYS AND COLLECTIVE MEMORY

Traversing the Royal Mile in Edinburgh, Scotland, provides another context, as does a walk through the historic Venetian Ghetto. In both locations, my photo-based urban diaries have shown attributes of today's urbanism that are often controversial, and it is not difficult to see why. Narrow streets might at first glimpse imply poverty and darkness, and multistory redevelopment might indicate poor living conditions and disease. But today's context is different: this is an informed era that can absorb both the positive and negative lessons of the past.

Height, density, and the use/control of land and public health in urban settings have evolved for a very long time. I found that my urban diary about Edinburgh cast light on this urban history of reinvention and renewal and helped me think more universally about how the

Figure 4.15

Figure 4.16

past, present, and future define urban development. As urban thinkers such as Sir Patrick Geddes once stressed, the real emphasis is on the power of continuous human settlement—and on inspiration gleaned from a dynamic city over time.[7] According to the Scottish architectural historian Miles Glendinning, the humble acceptance of the long-term reminds us that change is a constant, and that specific themes of long-term habitation can create broader ways of understanding the cyclical nature of urban reinvention.[8]

One reason for encouraging urban diaries is to help us understand that the rediscovery of the inner city is the *raison d'être* of many city dwellers today, and that dense urban cores are both increasing lifestyle choices and acting as economic drivers from the regional to international levels. We now tend to disfavor sprawl as a solution to overcrowded conditions, and stress instead old standbys such as increased height, cooperative living spaces, and smaller dwellings—but not everyone observing the associated changes is comfortable with what they see.

I have found through diary pathway walks in places like Edinburgh's World Heritage areas that our current ability to safely add urban density is reflective of lessons learned long ago, when overpopulated and unsanitary conditions within city walls eventually inspired new understandings of urban disease control. Within medieval Edinburgh, buildings as high as eleven to fifteen stories once flanked the High Street (Royal Mile) connecting Edinburgh Castle to Holyrood Palace.

What lessons emerge from buried medieval closes and formerly inhabited, now-forgotten building vaults of the Old Town? In a tour of the remaining portions of several abandoned underground medieval closes that have been covered by building foundations since the eighteenth century, I saw eerie parallels to today's reinvented urban alleys and laneways, aPodments (small units of congregate housing that share a communal kitchen), and live–work dwellings—medieval spaces evolving without the shadow of pestilence—back to the future, with a modern gloss.

Similarly, it was not hard to see how today's urban redevelopers can repopulate the shells of the past when opportunities for a more modern form of infill present themselves. In 2002, a fire destroyed a group of Edinburgh's Old Town tenements (termed a "rabbit warren" by firefighters) next to the historic Cowgate area. The Edinburgh-based development company Whiteburn Projects worked with planners, heritage groups, and the community to assemble eight formerly disparate properties and redevelop the area into a mixed-use venue including a new hotel and a grocery store.

In the end, the historical perspective presented by this sort of directed urban diary raises interesting questions about the nature of urban change and the way a global economy integrates with an evolving urban artifact. To an American observer from Seattle, one hometown image—the Starbucks logo—stood out. In figures 4.15 and 4.16, storied history and modern lifestyle communicate their "age value" to one another, along the Royal Mile and from a vaunted wide avenue of the New Town, respectively. Looking up from the New Town's George Street, midway between St. Andrew Square and Charlotte Square, medieval past and global future speak across the ages to their uniting element: human ingenuity and reinvention.

Pathway urban diaries can also highlight the public/private interfaces along streets, where an enhanced urban "look and feel" can derive from simple traditions of visual diversity. In another comparative effort, I illustrated the private-side faces presented to public view, emphasizing eclectic windows in Provence. This diary created a back-and-forth conversation between American facades (fig. 4.17) and their counterparts (fig. 4.18), contrasting often uneventful stylistic reserve and usually empty balconies with traditions of rich color and plantings, angular perspectives, and private spaces speaking outward to the street. In this context, I have asked: What if American cities legislated brighter color amid windows, filled balconies with green plants, and encouraged flags and hanging laundry? What if homeowner associations and rental contracts required vegetation and decoration of the interface with the street below?

CASSIS, FRANCE: "FINESSE OF THE AVENUE"

In another street-related urban diary, I focused more on how a weekend street closure has added ambience to a central, more commercial neighborhood in Cassis, France, because the underlying form from a simpler time emerges when the street becomes pedestrian-only. This is because the relationship between multiple urban elements is more apparent without the presence of the automobile.

In an important example of the potential use of a compiled urban diary from afar, the "finesse of the avenue" derived not just from the closure itself, but from the contextual tale that emerged while traversing

Figures 4.17 and 4.18   The facade conversation.

the particular road surface. To me, the Avenue Victor Hugo in Cassis told the stories surrounding its pavement and curbs. People walked the avenue between a small square-with-fountain and the quay, while the trees, awnings, and overhangs together cast the shadows that passers-by always need. The shiny, at-angle paving stones reflected the light in ways seldom seen on a street. And ambient noise seemed pleasant and appropriate, muffled perhaps by the envelope of finesse just described.

As noted, this experience in Cassis was a major reminder about how several factors can combine to create a "finesse of the avenue"—a noteworthy confluence of people (both natives and tourists), of physical aspects of the urban environment, and of the human senses of sight and sound. In short, natural, built, and human factors merged in a perfect storm of light, trees, stones, and scale. But, of course, it was not a storm at all—rather an exemplary venue to practice the "place decoding" called for in earlier chapters.

While Cassis is known as a fishing-village-turned-touristic-haven (and a departure point for visiting dramatic rock faces above the Mediterranean and remarkable inlets along coast, a short distance from Marseille), this urban diary was not a travelogue. Rather, it focused on the human impact of one of the simplest and most common municipal interventions: closure of a street to automobiles on market day, or during times of heavy use of a place (in this case, tourists gathering to board boats or visit the beach on a September Saturday). As a result, inherent and longstanding qualities of the place reemerged for the people.

Two comparison photos in this urban diary showed Cassis (via a useful, limited, comparison application of Google Street View) with full, off-season automobile access, and Cassis on that late morning in September 2014, when I photographed street use at a more human scale. Reviewing the two, it is not difficult to distinguish the ho-hum of figure 4.19 from the "finesse of the avenue" in figure 4.20.

The placemaking and tactical urbanism movements have already marshaled the festival imagery implied here in modern settings. We know that medieval townscapes and small streets are not necessary for recreating pedestrian-oriented public spaces or mixing and reenabling nonmotorized transportation modes. Experimental or permanent transformations such as New York City's Times Square pedestrian plaza are increasingly well known and on their way to attaining best-practice status for our cities and towns. In a place like Cassis, however, a remarkable pedestrian experience is about more than just cutting off the cars.

SEEING THE "FINESSE OF THE AVENUE"

Some places have magical elements that combine in unique, empowering ways and have an inordinate impact on the urban experience. I have written about those special locales in *Urbanism Without Effort*, inferring associated people-based criteria of comfort and scale.* Just as those criteria became clear for me in Neal's Yard in London, and in parts of the small, cohesive downtown blocks in Portland, Oregon, they reemerged with vigor in the Cassis experience.**

Cassis, France, on a September Saturday shows the essentials of everyday life—carried out in public with comfort and apparent ease. While some people are walking, others are selling, shopping, reading,

and attending to pets or to each other. These essentials stand out amid the merger of private and public, and the temporary compromise of the automobile. In my opinion, the "envelope of finesse" of light, trees, shade, and reflection, described above, worked a magic aura without over-designed intervention.

Courtesy of Google Street View

Figure 4.19

Figure 4.20

This urban diary excerpt amplifies my earlier statements and other summary quotations about urban observation. Communicating this "finesse of the avenue" through photographs is as valuable as the scholars' and thought leaders' views about successful urban attributes. Places with the look and feel of Avenue Victor Hugo, if interpreted in context, illustrate successful attributes of urban public spaces, and they help define the infrastructure and services that cities should equitably provide. It's a gut-level, observational process, which every one of us has the means to carry out in order to better understand the underlying makeup of successful city life.

* Charles R. Wolfe, *Urbanism Without Effort* (Washington, DC: Island Press, 2013).
** See two entries in the *myurbanist* blog: "Urban Radar and Finding Places of Scale," April 2, 2010, http://www.myurbanist.com/archives/1948; and: "Portland: Framing the Question of Place," May 15, 2011, http://www.myurbanist.com/archives/6227.

Looking for Juxtapositions: Bringing Drama to the Urban Diary

As noted in chapter 2, Gordon Cullen's epic early-1960s work described the visual experience of townscape views through an emphasis on "serial vision," and on present and emerging views that become revelations while moving from place to place.[9] More than Edmund Bacon, who focused his *Design of Cities* on similar experiential aspects framed by the built environment,[10] Cullen provided extensive typologies of architecture and street patterns through photographic example, concentrating on the experience of moving from place to place. For Cullen, passing through the built environment was full of tensions, delight, drama, and contrasts, specifically, the "drama of juxtapositions." I also arrived at the same term, *juxtapositions*, through my travel and pathway observations, and, as explained in the introduction, it is an essential element of the urban diary.

I believe that an enhanced sense of belonging and safety can result from the totality of our observations. For many years, my urban exploration has stressed an experiential approach to urban juxtapositions, overlaps, intersections, and all the other descriptors apparent in urban life.

This observational approach is valuable because of how it forces a self-realized immersion beyond reading the ever-evolving blogs and articles about best practices and others' sensations from afar. (See plate 22.)

I have thought a lot about such juxtapositions, and why they are points of context and focus—catalysts for today's urban dialogues. These observed overlays seem to force discussion of sudden and gradual change, generational differences, public and private preferences, mergers of cultures and business types, and mixing of land uses, transportation modes, and housing approaches. They are more than transitions, and reveal possible answers to questions about urban agendas and how urban change affects those who live and work nearby. Accordingly, they ultimately drive urban politics and professional services, and to find the better city we need to read it well in order to see where the juxtapositions are.

As the following photographs show, they are often in plain sight, in familiar patterns of overlap, or in layers. Notice a juxtaposition—and see debates about use of a place, flashpoints, and ripples in time—all of which are apparent in the spaces and human expressions of everyday life. Through these recordable teaching moments, we can often predict policy discussions, neighbor opposition, generational differences, and historical inequities in a way that can inspire a search for consensus, or even outright conflict and confusion.

Figure 4.21 is an early-evening rendition of an urban mixed-use project, under construction next to an abandoned house. Nearby streetlights cast shadows of branches against both existing buildings and the new construction. This urban juxtaposition spans natural and artificial light, trees, and houses in an evolving neighborhood.

Sometimes the built environment—so much a focus of day-to-day urban affairs—dwarfs in comparison to other, overlapping dimensions. In figure 4.22, the intensity of experience results from boats in the marine environment, the backdrop of weather conditions, and a mountain visible from the city. Such a scene is characteristic of cities ranked for their beauty or for their proximity to recreation and nature. Taking notice of the juxtapositions in this photograph embraces the assets of a place; the power of the image stems from the combination of its subjects, not any one component. The urban diarist finds value in the overlaps and blending of boats, sky, and mountain that create an inspirational experience, over and above viewing each overlapping element individually.

Figure 4.21

Figure 4.22

Figure 4.23

The contrast of old-versus-new, as seen in the evolving neighbor-hood in figure 4.21—is often a central overlay to any policy analysis or planning exercise. In one sense, as shown in figure 4.23—(the overlay of modern visitors on ancient Pompeii sidewalks), the basis for modern infrastructure readily appears in surviving examples from the distant past. While old-versus-new is perhaps the most direct juxtaposition in the city, it is an incomplete expression of all the interacting forces at play when something modern overlays a leftover from another time.

Although regulatory tools such as design review may attempt to define—and assure—authenticity, and essentially approach change as either an appropriate, compatible enhancement or an undesirable imposition, figures 4.24 and 4.25 introduce additional, complementary parameters. They show how analysis of change should be more qualita-tive and contextual, and should focus on the many overlays that are part of the evolution of urban space.

First, the ancient Roman amphitheater in Fréjus, France, displays restoration for uses, such as concerts, that are very different from its original purpose. Second, a new Starbucks fills a refurbished portion of the Rossio railway station in Lisbon, Portugal. However, not just old-versus-new, or physical structure, but several other forces at play in these

Figure 4.24

Figure 4.25

photographs invite analysis and discussion. For instance, how should a Roman arena be reused? Should an American coffee chain enhance (or compromise) the historic portal to a renowned capital city? These are questions—beyond old-versus-new—that the urban diary imagery of overlays, enhancements, and impositions continue to provoke around the world. Another example comes from the story of Rabat and Mdina.

WHAT JUXTAPOSITIONAL PHOTOGRAPHS REALLY SHOW

We often debate the supposed lifestyles and development patterns of suburb and city. But juxtapositional photographs help illustrate that sometimes a city looks like a suburb and a suburb looks like a city. That is the case below, with comparable imagery from across the world, and across urban history.

In the photograph, below, the foggy, high-rise skyline of Bellevue—a so-called suburb—contrasts with one of Seattle's oldest single-family neighborhoods in a particularly provocative way. I met this glowing vision of a "suburban" center (over which Seattle has no jurisdiction) amid Seattle's ongoing debates on how best to accommodate new building height and simultaneously achieve affordability, growth-related services, and infrastructure.

Figure 4.26

In figure 4.27, the fuzzy line between city and suburb is challenged even more directly, based on the literal translations of place-names dating back at least a thousand years. Mdina, Malta, the island country's historic hill town capital, contrasts with its surroundings, including the adjoining town of Rabat (to the left). In the Maltese dialect (substantially based on Arabic), "Mdina" (like the Arab *Medina*) means "city," and "Rabat" was derived from *dahiat*, the Arabic word for "suburb"—but, ironically, Mdina was eclipsed in size and encompassed by the larger Rabat long ago.

Figure 4.27

The age-old distinctions of urban boundaries and city walls matter less today in a physical sense, but both these photographs suggest that the political overlay of regions, cities, and neighborhoods still keep visible form, however counterintuitive. And this age-old juxtaposition of city and suburb, as well as their latent interrelationships, still dominates today's writing about cities.

Some revel in imagery of the decline of the suburbs and creative reinvention and retrofit; writings about resurgent suburban strategies in the face of city ascendance are now appearing regularly, including books by Ellen Dunham-Jones and June Williamson.* (Or even more recently, Jillian Glover's thoughtful reflection about suburbs as a laboratory for millennials to remake sprawl.)**

I prefer the universal spirit suggested by visually contrasting, and aligning, city and region—and the "ripple in time" that these photographs represent. The reason is that this documentary view shows that, however proximate, the land-use strategies of two places are uncoordinated. The observed juxtaposition might inform an urban diary about the virtues of regional government and cooperative solutions to issues of the day. Mdina and Rabat are place-names that have outlived their meaning in Malta, something we might consider for our own language of urbanism.

* Ellen Dunham-Jones, *Retrofitting Suburbia, Updated Edition: Urban Design Solutions for Redesigning Suburbs* (Hoboken, NJ: John Wiley & Sons, 2011); June Williamson, *Designing Suburban Futures: New Models from Build a Better Burb* (Washington, DC: Island Press, 2013).
** Jillian Glover, "Not All Young People Will Abandon Their Cars and Leave the Suburbs," *This City Life*, January 23, 2014, http://thiscitylife.tumblr.com/post/74355113571/not-all-young-people-will-abandon-their-cars-and.

In summary, many juxtapositions that frame urban form and experience are implicit in both the objective and the subjective city. Analysis and dialogue about overlaps and overlays can help avoid a divisive undercurrent to the ongoing refinement of urban best practices.

What we see every day drives thoughts, questions, policies, and plans. Images that depict the ambiguous edges of a modern settlement are catalysts beyond labels. They show urban juxtapositions that should take us beyond such traditional terms as *city*, *suburb*, *region*, and *neighborhood*, and instead focus on the forces that are common to all. Examples include the basics common to all urban areas—movement, settlement, home–work connectivity, and modes of travel.[11]

JUXTAPOSITIONS AND "INCONGRUITY"

Urban diaries often address specific subjects such as nature, building forms, streets, and transportation. As the last few stories reveal, these subjects also overlap and are juxtapositional. Consider how urban diaries might address juxtapositions of big versus small, and, taking from Berenice Abbott's multiple ways of conceiving skyscraper aesthetics,[12] spur deeper, more contextual discussion about allegations that something is "too big" or "out of scale," and about what our reference points and compromises should be.

One day, a colleague in my lawyer day job contacted me in search of an "expert" on the adverse impacts of height and scale. His client needed testimony asserting that a proposed development, flanking a current urban open space, would be "incongruous" with an existing parklike setting. This request for a recommendation—and its premise—was not unusual for a pending design-review process, which is often fraught with delay and obstruction by those opposed to change.

For many, a new project that will create dramatic contrast to existing building size and placement is the recipe for "incongruity." In this case, however, the assertion was the gateway to a far deeper discussion: should inquiry about an urban project address only surrounding building height and proportional architectural solutions (sometimes termed "density with grace")? In comparison, I considered all of the issues of Chicago's Millennium Park, where a classic and popular urban open space surrounded by tall buildings has compiled a multifaceted history of controversy, funding snafus, cost overruns, and debates about security practices and public access.[13] I concluded that the juxtaposition of "big versus small" was only the beginning.

Urban blending and any associated quest for balanced development are much broader topics than "incongruity" alone and deserve more than summary description. As I said to my colleague, the requested expert testimony risked subjective conclusions rather than the thoughtful analysis that governmental decision-makers would need. Once a potential urban overlap, overlay, or "juxtaposition" emerges, the search for harmony and agreement should travel far beyond matters of height and scale, and should be discussed in a comprehensive fashion, not reduced to a few of what lawyers call "conclusory" words.

Today, many "experts" opining on tall, "densifying" edges of public open space are more concerned with broader issues, such as funding mechanisms that pay for the open space and improvements, as well as other key urban "go-to" matters such as transportation and housing. This breadth of attention can lead to a very different view that rethinks "incongruity" not as a problem, but as the inevitable urban solution. In other words, the "incongruity" that some would cast as a soulless, uneven landscape of excessive height and bulk, becomes, for others, a treasure trove of irregular, provocative architecture and investment. This investment generates aesthetic and monetary capital to enhance, rather than detract from, the public realm nearby.

As often happens, consideration of these issues reminded me of something more fundamental and traditional—a mix of human imprints on the natural environment that I have illustrated in the past, a world away. In Iceland, I characterized much of what I saw there as an exceptional balance of human settlement and dramatic surroundings. Icelandic landscapes blend subtly with smaller towns and resurgent Reykjavik. Scaled scenes and stories merge nature, culture, and the built environment. My Iceland urban diary shows scaled expressions of urban settlement and transportation, along with dramatic examples of the longstanding human interplay with the raw elements of natural settings. (See plates 23 and 24.)

In these photographs, the visual juxtaposition of a fishing village and a glacier, of small buildings and sky, is, to me, nothing short of astounding. The harmony and agreement—the "congruity" that is the foil of this story—is clearly present where churches and outbuildings on the Snæfellsnes Peninsula honor natural surroundings with simplicity and scale.

But in the densifying city, can we, and should we, aspire to such purity implied by the words *congruity* and *incongruity?* How much should urban-redevelopment discussions, policies, and regulations embrace such resplendent and ideal visions? In this kind of scenario, a series of urban diary views can force a realistic conversation because, in a "densifying" urban core, the marketplace is often out of scale with more implementable development. The real cost of materials and the balance of profit complicate the limited aesthetic orientation suggested by the words *congruity* and *incongruity*.

The point of showing a vision as clear as the Snæfellsnes Peninsula is not to dwell in a nostalgia for a smaller scale overseas. Rather, by showing photographic examples of authentic harmony and agreement—at least as I see them—we can distinguish context, and distinguish the balance that humans still carry out in the raw landscapes of simpler places from the vocabulary of balance we often seek in our urban downtowns.

An urban diary can show how, when faced with a juxtaposition such as an "incongruous" urban development, the absolute extremes sought by proponents and detractors may be impossible to achieve. Compromises

AN URBAN DIARY OF JUXTAPOSITIONS

In an urban setting today, balance and "congruity" are not absolutes but rather they are end games with multiple meanings, dependent on context and careful reflection. Careful observation and recording allow for more meaningful reflection about the varied forces at play in urban settings. Accordingly, an urban diary of juxtapositions could easily further inform the many everyday overlaps apparent in cities around the world.

In five color plates, I offer a specific summary statement—and sometimes a lesson learned—about human scale, urban interactions with overlapping physical, sociocultural, natural, public, and private environments. Like my pictures of Iceland, this series presents an illustrated reminder of many of our baseline urban experiences, and some of the underlying forces that drive governments and communities toward consensus or opposition. (See plates 25–29.)

Figure 4.28

are inherently necessary when the discussion moves, as it inevitably does, toward the merger of public and private realms.

GLEANING INSIGHTS FROM SMALL DETAILS

Urban diary topics are as varied as the inspiration that we find in cities. While juxtapositions usually address holistic overlaps and how elements of a place relate to one another, the smaller scale sometimes holds appeal. Noticing the fine details—the kind of lighting that frames a place, the types of street trees, the use of paving stones or concrete in a neighborhood, the location of hydrants—can also offer insights into what is appealing or not about a city. Consider the example of the shutter. Like streets, doors, and windows, shutters stand at the intersection of public and private domains. A venerable urban feature with Greco-Roman origins, the shutter historically provided security, privacy, shading, and ornamental interface. Today, shutters provide the urban diarist with one of many ongoing opportunities to recreate a sense of place and to define the vibrant look and feel of city spaces.

In other examples, I have chronicled the "sit-able city" through photography, and I've queried through illustration when legal systems should allow individuals to sit, wait, or interact in public or private spaces.[14] Urban diaries can also be the collaborative effort of two or more people. In "Reading the Evolution of Places" some years ago, I created an urban diary across the world with a Venezuelan architect I had never met.[15]

A similar, fine-grain focus—the lasting impact of several site-design elements from 400 years ago—framed my final urban diary sample in a very deliberately chosen Paris neighborhood for several days in the winter of 2016. I selected a well-known residential square, the Place des Vosges in Paris, and rented an apartment. My goal was to assess the look and feel of life today in an urban space that has been an inspiration for the configuration of town squares throughout the world. I also intended the exercise to blend many issues of exploration and observation, e.g., history, collective memory, the human search for order, "ghosts," transitions, and juxtapositions.

The Place des Vosges is a public square with a legendary history. It was developed in the early seventeenth century by Henri IV as the Place Royale, on the site of a former royal palace, and as worker housing and display space for a nearby silk factory. The King's Pavilion and thirty-five other buildings symmetrically placed around the central open space all featured the same basic design elements, including slate roofs with distinct dormers, and uniform facades of white stone and red brick arranged over vaulted arcades. Some call it the world's first modern real estate development—based on the king ceding land to developers with conditions that they develop to specifications provided—while others term it an early example of more modern city-planning practice.

I did not choose the Place des Vosges as an elitist or overly romantic and nostalgic urban diary subject, nor was I mandating travel as necessary to the assessment of one's own city spaces. This sample is not intended as a public life study in the spirit of Whyte or Gehl.[16] Rather, I present it as a chronicle of an exemplary and foundational place, mindful that its uniform, planned appearance was never conceived to accommodate the mix of uses apparent in my photographs today. Rather, the Place des Vosges has organically evolved over time. While retaining the original form of the Place Royale, it carries a newer name that dates to the Napoleonic era. It is the epitome of how cities change, and as such it presents a variant of the "best" type of urbanism that I championed in *Urbanism Without Effort*: "the urbanism we already have," forever evolving. (See plate 30 and figures 4.29–4.31)

Actor/author Leonard Pitt's opening revelation in his book *Paris: A Journey Through Time* is worth recalling for anyone interested in how urban change occurs: as he acknowledges, his early assumptions of a single homogenous plan behind Parisian landmarks and street patterns were entirely wrong.[17] Generally speaking, the streets and landmarks in today's Paris weren't born of a single plan or program, but rather

Figure 4.29

Figure 4.30

they resulted from the familiar, organic factors of population growth and in-migration, commercial and industrial change, and *"chance, fate, accident, greed, and the individual choices of ordinary citizens"* (emphasis added).[18]

Pitt identifies the Place des Vosges as a prime example of organic change that has occurred not only on-site but also elsewhere in the city due to events that occurred in the Place—an important lesson from history. He observes how the inadvertent consequences of a sixteenth-century public tragedy in the Place ultimately shaped the enhancement of

Figure 4.31

the Louvre and its related structures, gardens, and open spaces, including the Tuilleries Gardens and eventually the Place de la Concorde and
the Champs Elysees, that then independently evolved over time: "Place
des Vosges would never have seen the light of day were it not for the
fatal injury suffered by Henri II when his opponent's lance pierced his
eye during a jousting tournament held at the Hôtel des Tournelles in
1559. In her grief, his queen, Catherine de Medici, ordered the palace
demolished, thus opening the place for the Place des Vosges. The ripple
effect of this accident continued to shape Paris for centuries."[19]

Today, in more modern parlance, the Place features mixed-use, private surroundings around a central open space. Observing the Place
and creating an associated urban diary enabled me to examine features
of urban life that many cities attempt to emulate today, including a central, walkable open space; dense, colorful surroundings; and an ordered
symmetry that looks very much the same as it did 400 years ago. Even
early in its history, the Place's already well-emulated form and function

influenced major public squares in other cities (e.g., the Plaza Mayor in Madrid), and today it can provide any urban diarist with an inspirational prototype of form and function for any discussion of urban redevelopment models.

A SAMPLE URBAN DIARY ABOUT THE PLACE DES VOSGES

My approach to documenting the Place followed a partial adaptation of the **LENS method** identified in chapter 3, as follows:

> **Urban diary type:** Journal, Travel Guide, Photo essay, Comparative Analysis
>
> **Starting point:** 11 Place des Vosges, Paris
>
> **Pre-diary overview:** Used Google Maps and Google Street View and several guidebooks and historical overviews. Further orientation from photographs from late-2014 visit.
>
> **Mode of travel:** Walking, coupled with both directed and drift techniques.
>
> **Initial goals:** Orientation; determining development forms in area and getting a better understanding the human–urban interface in and around the Place as evolved over time. Observing how, in fulfilling daily needs (as set out at the beginning of chapter 4), people interact with different spaces, particularly inside and outside the arcades, accesses to the Place (via streets and the walk through the Hôtel de Sully courtyard), and on and near dirt paths within the fenced park at center, and with respect to areas where automobiles are allowed. General notation of look, feel, take-away sensation. From a *qualitative* perspective for comparison's sake: What is similar and what is missing in other cities? How is the Place a welcoming place for people in ways that we do or do not see at home? What is the surviving and ongoing role of the uniform development pattern, first incentivized through the reward of land for compliance with the king's design criteria in the Henri IV era, and what is its role in an evolving city?
>
> **LENS parameters:** Diary began with photo documentation using handheld camera at doorway to apartment. Photographs obtained

to assess qualities of day-to-day experience and assessment of the following:

Overview

Keystone, overview observations, for example, a linear portrait, a bird's-eye view from a hill or tall building where possible or a skyline view
Diagonal views across open space, by day or night, displayed symmetry and relationship of original arcaded facade to open space and surroundings.

People–Place Focus

People–place interactions wherever relevant: illustrations of relationships with surroundings, activities, and, where available, identities of people portrayed
This was an important parameter, as the observation of how people come together in Parisian spaces is a time-honored tradition with qualities that are imitated worldwide.

Will you search for crowds and associated opportunities to mingle and become part of those assembled?
Key views of center of Place display human-use patterns.

Diary Subject Matter and Inquiry

Will you seek out public spaces such as parks, squares, dedicated building spaces, and markets? How will you move within and around them?
See above; diagonal and circumnavigation.

Role of transportation modes: Primarily pedestrian but automobiles noted on periphery and circumnavigating open space.

Role of nature, generally: Trees and limited plantings apparent in open space.

Role of light and color generally: Photographs show the importance of the red brick to overall view.

Role of history: symbols, "ghosts"; building stratigraphy, monuments; what is traditional, inherent?
See narrative above and below.

Role of change: observations of identifiable change in the urban landscape
N/A

Notation of how places survive differently
Place appears much as it once did, leading to questions of why, and whether this is mandated, or simply preferred.

Where public/private spaces meet or overlap: convergence points (corners), adequacy of sidewalk frontage space, juxtapositions/ incorporations of old/new, nature/built, color, enhancement of dense residential frontages (doors, windows balconies)
Photographs show internal arcade experience; see below.

Role of height and scale: observations of compatibility or lack thereof under existing conditions or new construction; compromise to the presence of nature and light
An overwhelming sense of symmetry; constant awareness of relative darkness of arcades.

Accessory features: street furniture to accommodate human needs (shelter, sitting, watching, privacy), fences, hedges (cf. safety)
Most apparent in open space benches, hedges.

Spontaneity and everyday urbanism (graffiti, unregulated signage, temporary or pop-up uses, unintended uses)
Homeless use of arcades at night.

Governmental Specifics

Safety parameters: Crime Protection through Environmental Design (CEPTED): Barriers, lighting, eyes on the street, mode separation that allow for seamless contextual traditions between different transit modes.
Fences in open space, open space locked at night, arcade lighting.

Role of government intervention in permitting, does it help/hinder your experience?
Architectural controls.

Provisional end point: 11 Place des Vosges

Conclusions and use: *Assemble photographs in a way that can be presented to inspire and show what is possible, in context—what might be adaptable, what not. Show people in the context of a particular urban space.*

The major lessons include the overpowering role of the surviving square and building configuration. While efforts to restore and maintain the Place in recent years (rescuing the neighborhood from decline) have readily observable aesthetic benefits, it is clear from observation that many layers of complexity remain. In a place full of architectural beauty, the homeless sleep and paramilitary soldiers demonstrably protect a synagogue. Here, Raban's *Soft City*, the city of dreams, clearly has a place alongside physical form, no matter how classic or outstanding that form may be.

The Place today ranges in use from cafés to residences, with a park dominating the interior, locked at night. Various businesses, other than cafés, also fill the first floor areas; the majority use is clearly art galleries and vendors. Other uses include hotels, several galleries, a *parfumerie*, and other general shops. Two national monuments flank two corners, the Victor Hugo House and the Hôtel de Sully. A synagogue (that fronts on an adjoining street) is located midway down the east side.

While the Place retains its remarkable symmetry and looks very similar to how it has looked during other times in its history, there are other facets that are ripe for place-decoding. Cars flank the fenced park area and create a division of the archways from any green space. The covered perimeter around the square creates ready shelter for all, including the two or three homeless who sleep around the square in boxes and sleeping bags or blankets. Also, the several doors leading off of the Place mask whole worlds in themselves, with private courtyards and residential accesses locked away from public view or access. I know from experience that a loud party in one of those spaces is somehow an invasive surprise. A key takeaway is that the symmetry of the space—the preserved layout with a unique history—becomes a focal point for observing the randomness of city life. The order is so clear that it is initially comforting; the human interplay (if one chooses to focus on it) is a set of mini-dramas, almost begging for interpretation. It is not the monumental space of later Paris, nor one devoted to public assembly, like the Place de la République.

The Place example is something that at first seems readily exportable, but raises on its face complex questions regarding maintenance and regulation. While the noted symmetry is initially comfortable and uniform, human activity—so important to a city—seems a disturbance, an invasion. Unmaintained facades and chipped stone in an archway raise issues of repair, and park activity in the center is distinct from that around existing structures. In the end, the Place des Vosges is a remarkable artifact and symbolic of the contrast between the physical city of without, and the personal city of within, and all of the forces at play in an urban place.

My sample urban diaries are suggestive, not prescriptive, and the **LENS** method provides broad guidance. The diary should set out observed examples of what resonates with and inspires the diarist to portray or define his or her personal city. Depending on the diary's purpose and presentation, it could be in its quintessential form descriptive or illustrative, but it could also be reactive, reflective, oppositional, supportive, idealistic, comparative, disdainful, or some combination of these qualities. In several of the diary-like vignettes presented above, I have chosen an alternative that honors juxtapositions, overlays, and what I believe are simple truths of how cities evolve.

Behind any method of urban exploration there is also a remarkable truth in Jane Jacobs's advice—to just get out and look around—that encourages the nudging and nurturing of our senses. Equally critical is Rob Forbes's inclination toward jump-starting the observation process by seeing and photographing curve and color. Every neighborhood surrounding has something worth noticing and worth using as an example of one component of the better city.

Despite the many examples of "how to observe" available across the disciplines, adapting others' exploration techniques describing how to prepare an urban diary may seem overly directive. Especially if the urban diary will serve as a practical tool after more creative,

immersive first steps, the challenge becomes rationalizing the subjective and assigning systematic parameters to what should arguably be
a personal and random affair. After all, the *dérive* of the Situationists
is, by its very definition, the opposite of a cookie-cutter approach. The
next chapter considers how cities may combine a personal exploratory
and observational approach with municipal processes and developing
technologies.

FROM URBAN DIARIES TO POLICIES, PLANS, AND POLITICS

—

Everyone can practice integral urbanism, not just
planners and urban designers. It entails discovering
what is integral to a place—its DNA, unique qualities,
gifts—and honoring them. . . . Once these gifts are
identified, we can connect the dots to strengthen them
and engage in urban acupuncture to liberate the life
force of a city, allowing it and us to truly thrive.

— NAN ELLIN
"The Tao of Urbanism"[1]

The city is an undeniably human creation, full of our emotions, impressions, and experiences. Yet the policy and regulatory processes that govern the city are often evidence-based. Unless a viewpoint or submittal is validated by experts, these processes may preclude the ability of an individual to have a meaningful impact on urban change. In official deliberations, as elected officials have often told me, the potential human experience is underemphasized in favor of tangible structures, cross-sections, and models.

Accordingly, how can we re-infuse process with all-important attention to the human experience? How to account for the irrational and unplanned, for the juxtapositions that infuse a city with energy, both positive and negative? In a practical sense, how can all this come together in a meaningful way to reform and reframe our process for civic decision making? We are just beginning to scratch the surface of possibilities for urban diaries and related collaborative efforts with toolkits, smart-city "data-driven" approaches, and new approaches to long-term planning efforts.

Converting idealistic notions of better cities into concrete and discernable results is a significant challenge—essentially demanding a move from plan to action. The subjective, creative, emotion-based approaches discussed here seldom convert easily to the language of land-use applications, plan review, public hearings, and appeal processes, other than by narrative testimony or photographic exhibits. The rational processes of democratic decision making often reduce matters to text-laden decision criteria that emphasize code compliance, neighborhood compatibility, and environmental and traffic impacts. In fact, this necessary search for objectivity may purposefully deemphasize emotional response, urban traditions, or equitable outcomes.

The system, therefore, needs to be reinvented from within, taking advantage of the tools and examples discussed in the preceding chapters. This reorientation need not be as daunting as it may sound, especially if, in the end, we are discussing urban diaries as a complement, or supplement, to the conventional regulatory process. If urban diaries become public comment, equivalent to written or oral testimony, or are used as submittals for discussion during formal or informal mediation, then they will come into their own as colorful, illustrative, and demonstrative adjuncts to existing forums for decision making and dispute resolution. Urban observation will then be more than the purview of the dilettante, or fodder for elicited photography or app-based expressions.

Technology provides new tools of participation in our surroundings and a legion of sources and opinions about how best to experience the city. From casual smartphone camera use to participatory photography and mapping, mini-ethnographies, oral histories, and "now and then" nostalgia, ideas and approaches for urban diaries can be readily acquired online, at meet-ups, or organizational events. So many approaches, without cross-references, provide no central organization about how our personal urban experiences can meaningfully be put to work; useful precedent from other disciplines is often unacknowledged, and the end game is often unclear.

We may resolve to learn from such technology-based tools, but on the other hand we less often see cohesive organizational strategies for putting "notable/sensational" media and blog stories to work. Raising awareness is good, observation and contextual understanding is better, but the best outcomes will result when we move beyond observation for observation's sake. We should incorporate more visual urban diary–like documentation of human need and routine into the evidence that forms the basis for civic decision making.

In legislative hearings as well as quasi-judicial hearings, the use of photographs is already standard. In more-formal settings, rules govern the steps that must be taken to enter such photographs into a record. In law school evidence class, students learn the hearsay rule, which requires a courtroom witness to have firsthand knowledge of the truth of an assertion. Budding lawyers also master the rules for authenticating photographs for use by judges and juries, the principles of which usually apply to the less formal administrative process as well. At the core, the rules often address some elements of authenticity, such as the date and location of the photograph, and the identity of the photographer or source. If a photograph can be reasonably sourced and identified, and has relevance to the matter under discussion or review, then its use is usually not a problem.

We need to better wed the subjective, soft city—the personal, observed city—with the city of decision-makers and the projects presented by the marketplace. This combination presents a considerable challenge and requires that we merge "rationality with imagination, the prosaic with the dream world, the planned with the unexpected. . . ."[2] Here, urban diaries can lead the way as exemplary, inspirational, three-dimensional portraits of the most authentic and suitable visions of improved daily lives for the constituents of elected officials—urban residents themselves.

And, of course, better cities will emerge when decision-makers see that these portraits align with marketplace proposals. As part of the "Future Freo" visioning process in Fremantle, Australia, I watched Mayor Brad Pettitt present a Powerpoint narrative on potential future development strategies for his city after he'd made a Northern European study tour. Mayor Pettitt's approach suggests that elected officials could compile—and perhaps present—urban diaries on a regular basis, consistent with the ideas set out here.

In recent years, the real estate market has seen significant value in the walkable, compact city that is often the inevitable focus of urbanism photographs and associated urban diaries. The internet teems with images of streetcars and bicycles, walkable environments and healthy, exercise-oriented urban living, with plenty of shared transportation alternatives. But is this urbanism the inevitable result of choices made by municipal governments and the real estate marketplace? In short, can photographic imagery—as both art and archive—indeed help change cities for the better?

Blogs that emphasize photography advocate for sustainable cities and livability through imagery of amenities such as separated bike lanes, public transit, and walkable neighborhoods. In my view, the greatest communication asset in such urban blogs is the use of color, angle, light, shadow, and night settings to send inviting, moving portrayals of urban revitalization. Such imagery, if presented in context, often provides motivation for policy-makers to undertake their own explorations of how to move from plan to action.

Questions of authenticity also require that the in-person impressionistic be distinguished from sole reliance on the virtual. Articles and blogs about urban development feature "observations" about urban solutions, with depictions of places that the authors have never actually visited in person. The imagery comes from public domain sources such as Flickr, Shutterstock, or Instagram, or from desktop travel via Google Earth and Google Street View. Arguably, this easy accessibility expands the reach of both reader and writer. However, such "virtual visits only" are likely insufficient for the local input sessions, meetings, and hearings addressed here.

Practical Roles for Urban Observation and Urban Diaries

Many city-planning, placemaking, and development processes increasingly use photography in innovative ways to inform policy and design outcomes. Current approaches often employ a professional photographer, an architect, or an urban planner to create community imagery. This could easily be a first step toward integrating and assembling resident-generated photographs that capture observations from the community itself. Such photo-centric urban diaries, as discussed in this chapter, have many potential roles in improving city outcomes, from providing information as a form of crowd-sourced data to being formally used to analyze and prioritize community wants and needs.

————————————— ABOUT VIRTUAL VISITS

Virtual alternatives to the more rigorous first-person exploration of a place, like Google Street View, sometimes create
hybrid forms of urban observation. Some artists and photographers,
such as Doug Rickard (subject of *Doug Rickard: A New American
Picture*),* have created "diaries" premised on social commentary,
a removed form of the engagement mentioned earlier vis-à-vis the
websites *Overheard in New York* and *Humans of New York*. Similarly,
Bill Guffey created *The Virtual Paintout*, a blog premised on paintings from Google Street View images from around the world.** In
another New York effort, Justin Blinder's *Vacated*, profiled certain
locations, where, during the Bloomberg administration, vacant lots
or older buildings were "gentrified" by new development.† He then
took advantage of Google Street View's irregular update schedule to
show virtual cross-sections of new and old, such as completed and
half-completed buildings merged together as one.

While courtroom rules should not apply to such new media advancements, we might nevertheless pause and consider the risks of virtual
visits and secondary sources when advocating for change in a more
formal setting, such as before municipal decision-makers. Overreli-
ance on such sources may encourage artistic license best reserved for
even more creative endeavors.

I have experimented with a comparison of images from Google
Street View with personal, street-level photographs. In one example,
on a Seattle arterial, both images suggest a partially residential area
now used for small businesses. But then I ask: Are they equally reli-
able depictions for seeing the better city?

Figure 5.1

As is often the case on Google Street View, for privacy purposes certain items are obscured, such as personal names and some building details. This vagueness dims clarity, leaving an outline, a two-dimensional framework that invites more speculation than in-person observation would allow. Are the business uses freestanding, or attached to residences? Is the signage permitted? Is on-site parking allowed? Is this a residential area in transition? Are we witnessing a harbinger of suburban decay?

Figure 5.2

From a personal photo—one taken while actually being present in a place—the maturity of the businesses is clear, and the specific professional services—an acupuncturist and an optician—are all legible. The photo tells us of a sale on eyeglasses and, upon closer examination, also shows the nature of adjacent businesses. As the photographer, and with my personal knowledge of the neighborhood, I know that this area has long contained a mix of uses under appropriate zoning. It stands within part of a vital, largely walkable urban neighborhood of smaller houses and modernizing businesses, amid a post–World War II "neighborhood unit" configuration.

In fairness, Google Street View provides the essence of the in-person story, and the quality of the pictures almost matches the personal versions. Joint use of Google Maps and further internet research would bring a remote researcher even closer to the "truth." However, the removed Google Street View artist could easily spin a tale of intrigue and speculation, while the more literal, experiential local street photographer, with real local knowledge, might tell 'a story of urban reinvention.

> While I may disfavor the purely virtual approach as creating urban diary components, the value of Google Street View visits may be useful for providing overall context for comparison. When they are appropriately cast, easily accessible and sometimes fuzzy depictions will not compromise the intended final message, assuming they appear alongside in-person views. Still, virtual visits should be treated with care and circumspection, as a two-dimensional framework is by nature incomplete.
>
> * See: David Campany, *Doug Rickard: A New American Picture* (New York: Aperture, 2012); see also: http://www.dougrickard.com/a-new-american-picture/.
> ** For examples of Bill Guffey's paintings, see: http://virtualpaintout.blogspot.com.
> † Justin Blinder's cross-sections appear at: http://projects.justinblinder.com/Vacated.

The urban diary can serve a valuable function, even in the absence of a formal invitation from city officials to the public to provide organized input through a submittal process. Urban diaries can serve as a form of self-education, helping people to understand the diversity and complexity of the places where they live or work. Urban diaries can highlight the multiple perspectives about what constitutes a "good" or "bad" place, and they can expand individual and collective appreciation and knowledge by unlocking personal stories or experiences.

Cities from Austin, Texas, to Vancouver, Canada, to Adelaide, Australia, are showing how city-planning, development, and design processes can benefit from photographs taken by people living in the communities where urban planners, designers, developers, and politicians all perform their work. In these cities, the urban diary-style tools allow community members to advocate for the city they want to protect, to cultivate, or to emulate. There are myriad ways in which both community members and cities—working separately or in tandem with stakeholder groups—can experiment with approaches for integrating imagery of experiences and observations of places into urban-development processes.

Through an urban diary, persons or groups can provide an informal input into city projects and thus enhance the flow of discussion on an issue with an elected official, or enable an urban planner to better understand and visualize an issue raised in a conversation about a planning proposal or city strategy. Community groups already use this general approach to highlight select experiences and problems in the urban setting.

In Seattle, several nongovernmental organizations use photography to share information about issues with a broad audience and to demonstrate how photography is an effective tool for visually communicating citizen concerns, values, and experience of place. For example, "Facing Homelessness: Homeless in Seattle" is a Facebook page that shares portraits of people experiencing homelessness. While not a robust urban diary, this is one example of capturing photos of people's experiences in cities in order to raise awareness of an issue and to advocate for change and support. Similarly, the Blue Earth Alliance and Braided River are Seattle-based organizations that use documentary photography to inspire positive change. Blue Earth Alliance concentrates on documentary storytelling on environmental and social issues, while Braided River uses large-format books to protect wild places by "inspiring action to protect wild places through images and stories that change perspectives."[3]

The urban diary also provides a positive and proactive method for people to engage with the life of their city and their changing surroundings. As noted, public comment processes tend to seek conventional written input, and while elicited photography may not appear as a pre-authorized form of submittal, a photo-centric urban diary could enhance traditional land-use or design review processes. If used proactively, and not as a tool of delay, the urban diary can provide illustrations that complement written or oral submissions, assisting community members with effectively and efficiently articulating ideas or knowledge for decision-makers, whether they be urban planners or politicians. In some instances, the act of providing visual testimony may enhance the public record by forcing a neighbor to think positions through, or to argue for solutions that can be seen elsewhere.

Under a proactive approach, if a city government does not specifically solicit photographic examples, a resident might provide an independent submittal. For example, in Melbourne, Australia, anyone can participate at a council meeting by providing materials—including a Powerpoint presentation—earlier on the day of the scheduled meeting. Also, a citizen can, at the meeting, take a limited time to present to the committee on the chosen issue. Such processes provide an appropriate opportunity to the urban diarist to highlight existing conditions, potential problems, and preferred outcomes, as well as to enhance potential for the urban diary to inform decision making.

The urban diary can provide an informal input into city projects that monitor change or evaluate existing qualities for future improvement. Strategic-planning projects and processes are most likely to benefit from unsolicited input in the form of an urban diary that highlights concerns or preferences. Neighborhood planning is a process that encourages greater citizen engagement, and is also a grassroots approach to managing growth by inviting community members to be involved in the planning process. These participatory efforts have great potential to benefit from the urban diary—with community members using tools to highlight places that work well or are valued or otherwise require attention through policy, plan, or regulation, or that could benefit from examples from other locations. (See the Urban Storytellers website, briefly discussed in chapter 2.)

Local-character or historic-resource studies, such as the Redmond, Washington, example that follows in this chapter, can also benefit from urban diaries that highlight significant social connections to places, as well as the design, architectural, or landscape features of streets or neighborhoods. Such information can provide additional data input to character-based projects by highlighting areas that are valued or considered to be unique by the community, as well as types of development perceived either to complement or to undermine these places.

While many projects will engage professionals to conduct place-based research, such as on-site audits that review site capabilities and conditions, the urban diary can complement staff or consultant efforts by integrating local knowledge. Several toolkits are available for communities to undertake audits on a vast range of subjects, including walkability, sea-level rise, urban water management, neighborhood character, street redesign, and landscape studies. Certain examples, identified in chapter 2 in the "Assessment Toolkits and Digital Storytelling" section, provide advocacy approaches for informing authorities about improvement needs.

These toolkits often include a checklist of elements for community members to consider and incorporate. Assessment checklists could easily add an urban diary as a significant enrichment to data input intended

Figure 5.3   Residential input in the making.

to truly illuminate conditions on the ground for local communities. The Neighbourhood Walkability Checklist by the National Heart Foundation of Australia is a good example. The checklist encourages residents to document and photograph the walking conditions of their neighborhood, and it includes a template letter for sending this information to the local council.[4] The toolkit approach is also applicable in the context of broader city strategies and long-term plans, such as policies regarding urban forests or open spaces, city identity or branding initiatives, and placemaking projects. Chapter 2 identified select examples,[5] and additional elaborations appear below.

In particular, the urban diary provides a unique way for residents or community groups to connect with decision-makers or project teams, as well as engage with the broader public about urban experiences and issues. City leaders and decision-makers increasingly use social media to engage more directly with their constituents. Facebook, Twitter, and Instagram allow politicians to share information about projects they are advocating for, as well as tap into public perspectives. Social media also provides a platform where developers, architects, and urban planners can share projects, gain public input, and gain innovative ideas from examples of design and policy approaches. To architect Marc Kushner of HWKN, "Instagram, Facebook, and Twitter are fomenting the biggest revolution in architecture since the invention of steel, concrete, and the elevator. It is a media revolution."[6]

Kushner believes social media is creating a fundamental shift in power from established critics and tastemakers to the public—"the people who actually use architecture." Until recently, architects did not have a "truly unfiltered means" to hear the public's perspectives on their projects. The instantaneous communication made possible by social media has broken these barriers down, allowing people to consume architecture and engage in conversations free from geographical constraints: "Today, every single person who lays eyes on a building can be at once a user, an architectural photographer, and a critic with a public forum. . . . For the first time in history, architects can hear the public."[7] In a 2014 TED Talk, Kushner explained how, historically, the impact of a particular building on architectural practice took a long time to assess because of long feedback times in accounting for human experience, something now accelerated by the immediacy of social media: "When we take a picture of a building, and we share it with our friends, and we leave our comments on a building, we're short-circuiting our collective memory and we're telling the world about novelty, about innovation in architecture, so that we can finally move past traditional, staid responses to the places where we all live. That opens up a world of experimentation for the buildings where we spend our time."[8]

Methods of sharing—as diverse as Facebook, Twitter, Instagram, Flickr, or a website, videos on Vimeo or YouTube, or city sound recordings or oral commentary on SoundCloud—offer increased opportunities to connect with elected officials, as well as designers, urban planners, and other city policy-makers, and they can showcase ideas for improved outcomes or otherwise highlight issues, community values, or priorities. Sharing can proceed individually or via a group with a common interest. In a related, media-initiated approach, the *Guardian* often has a city resident take over one of its Instagram accounts and facilitate uploads to accompany a variety of news and feature stories about a given city.[9]

Social media provides an expanded platform in contrast with submitting an urban diary to a single government department, and this method has great potential for informing better city outcomes by allowing for this public feedback into projects, even when it is not required or requested by decision-makers. These social media platforms offer an opportunity for people to engage via the urban diary (whether it be in photographic, video, or sound format), by sharing, commenting, and "liking" to reflect a broader collective opinion.

In addition to the use of social media in Seattle described above, several other community groups share photos on their Facebook and Twitter accounts in order to highlight both poor experiences in the public realm and also good urban design examples from elsewhere. Touting alternative ideas through social media increasingly raises public awareness and education, and it alerts a range of professionals as to public perspectives.

Photography: Generating Interest, Crowd-Sourcing, and Smart Cities

While cities are increasingly crowd-sourcing information by asking residents to provide verbal input to generate ideas for the city's planning projects, photography is often used only as a "fun" or engaging method to make people aware of or become involved in a project, without any further purpose. It is often unclear how photographs and commentary provided by the community inform decision-makers about what the community knows, wants, or doesn't want.

However, a handful of cities around the world have experimented with applying urban diary–style components to enable the public to participate more fully in projects and help shape outcomes. Although new ways of engaging with architecture and cities using emerging social media are in their infancy, such methods, as highlighted by Marc Kushner, will evolve as we better understand the value of the urban diary to expand collective knowledge and capture diverse perspectives that can enrich decision making.

THE POTENTIAL OF PHOTOGRAPHY TO INFORM

Embracing new processes for photographic input will likely make better use of local expertise and community-based evidence. The visual narratives provided through urban diaries allow greater authenticity by integrating local knowledge that reflects the desires and needs of the people who live in an affected area. This knowledge will assist city decision-makers and enhance their ability to translate imagery and complementary commentary into better policy, design, and development outcomes.

The following examples show how encouraging residents to share their individual experiences of a city via an urban diary approach can raise the level of engagement and public participation in urban projects or city issues. Possibilities include generating interest in a chosen project and crowd-sourcing visual data, as shown in Vancouver's example. Seeking shared photographic expression can also be useful for expanding participation in a process to include people with diverse perspectives, such as children, the elderly, those with limited time, or people who are not comfortable with the local language, public speaking, or written commentary.

Example: Urban Diary to Generate Interest in a Project
(What Do You Picture — City of Vancouver, 2012)
As part of the city of Vancouver's 2012 "What Do You Picture" program, a community-planning photo contest invited community members to submit neighborhood photos, add comments, and view and rate other people's images.[10] The platform could be seen in both map view (and searched through a range of categories) and in thumbnail views that showed image ratings. Participants were asked: "What are the great places and spaces in your neighbourhood? This could include great views, special buildings, parks, and even the people that you feel express the uniqueness of your community." The city further invited people to "Show us the hidden gems, your favourite routes, the places you like to visit, or the ones you choose to avoid, in this community planning photo contest. Submit your favourite photos of Grandview-Woodland, Marpole, and the West End, and we will choose 18 winners."

Cities can easily extend Vancouver's approach by inviting the public to help identify issues or priorities and asking respondents to share their observations and knowledge as a basis for plans, project information, or decision making that can now include fuller-fledged community visioning. This form of outreach or involvement alerts public officials to features of a city not previously noted, and may provide the basis for policy changes or regulatory reform. I suggest the increased use of this directed outreach for particularly important urban issues such as affordability, homelessness, and reducing the number of parking spaces required for new construction. Compelling examples include people who are living in vehicles and are in need of emergency parking locations or shelters, and allowing the use of underutilized commercial parking areas for purposes other than originally intended, such as park-and-rides for nearby public transit stops or stations.

In more-focused outreach, cities have invited community members to submit photos showing their observations, values, likes and dislikes, or exemplary images from elsewhere that can serve as local models. Ultimately, such information can be integrated into documents, reports, and presentations as accessible and reflective of the perspectives of the community (rather than use of photos by professional photographers or by built-environment professionals, which may appear more directed than participatory). Outcomes, such as appropriate building form; preferred use of sidewalks, streets, and unique places; and overall compatibility of neighborhood elements can achieve greater authenticity because photos directly reflect the insights of people who live or use the spaces.

Smart-city approaches such as crowd-sourcing data inputs and collaborative mapping can dovetail with individual photographic contributions to city-sponsored efforts. Photographs are complementary to mapping (e.g., through Google Maps or Instagram), which creates opportunities to map local data to be shared across a suite of projects or initiatives. For example, a general urban diary / shared map platform can allow the same images and commentary to be used for a diversity of projects, ranging from strategic, long-term planning to urban-design policy.

Certain types of shared photo requests, like pictures of urban waterways to inform projects relating to flooding, water quality, and sea-level rise—can double as community education and knowledge-seeking projects, cutting time and costs for cities and decision-makers. One article summarized three approaches in Dublin, Ireland, that included diary-based photography and GPS tracking.[11] These approaches focused on residents' responses to city features; collaborative urban awareness walks where participants used stickers to identify places of interest; and a group website with multiple entries about tracked routes, photographs, and city features that participants found relevant to their daily experience. Such a combination of photo requests and education may provide a simple and efficient means of building evidence that is not otherwise readily available, and it could easily be extended to urban wildlife initiatives or enforcement projects.[12]

As mentioned in the introduction, in recent years a variety of smartphone apps for reporting issues in need of fixing (often termed "find it, fix it") have been pioneered to enable citizens to connect efficiently with city government. These apps allow reporting of something in need of immediate attention, such as graffiti, potholes, or illegal dumping, by taking a photo and tagging the location. Reports are sent directly to the specific city department responsible for maintenance. Apps such as BOS:311 in Boston and Philadelphia's 311 have established a precedent for using citizen photography to highlight city issues affecting the enjoyment of city life, and they can result in improved infrastructure and living conditions.[13] These services illustrate the potential for addressing longer-term issues affecting a changing city; they can elevate communication beyond the reporting of immediate nuisances to the most experiential encounters with the built environment. These apps have the potential to empower people to express their observations and insights visibly and share them directly with elected officials and other city policy-makers.

Example: Crowd-Sourcing Visual Data
(Imagine Austin — CodeNEXT — Shaping Austin)
Imagine Austin (2012), the city's thirty-year plan for the future, "is based on Austin's greatest asset: its people," with ideas and contributions from the community.[14] The plan establishes a vision for how the city can grow in compact and connected ways while addressing quality of life through investment in the creative economy and advancing healthy, affordable living. CodeNEXT (2015–2016) is the city of Austin's Land Development Code revision initiative, intended to update how city land can be used and developed with sensitivity to community input.[15] The project evolved in collaboration with residents, businesses, and institutions to ensure that land-use standards and regulations align with community values.

Austin's approach exemplifies how an urban diary can be developed by a community, with applicability to neighborhood or historic character projects, and updates to comprehensive plans, zoning codes, and urban-design guidelines. A self-styled urban diarist, or groups of diarists, can plug existing efforts into an Austin-style process. This way, the soft city of self-generated, evocative photography might be married to more refined, contemporary city-led innovation.

Members of the Austin community were also invited to participate in generating information and imagery about their neighborhoods through another outreach program, "Community Character in a Box."[16] The city provided a do-it-yourself toolkit and suggested ways that community members could capture images of the assets, constraints, and opportunities for improvement in their neighborhood (which was encouraged in small groups), as documented both via photos and marked on maps.[17] The toolkit provides team instructions for how to take photos and submit them to the project, and it explains their intended use.

The more important instructions are similar to elements of photography discussed in chapter 3 in the "How to Photograph: Helpful Hints" section; they suggest photographing while walking, not driving; putting the camera on the highest-quality setting; thinking about composition; emphasizing residential and commercial buildings, sidewalks, streets, and unique places. The final page of the toolbox instructions, containing well-framed example photographs, also suggests attention to landmarks, architectural styles, setbacks and building–street relationships, and compatibility of nearby buildings to one another. Moreover, the toolkit narrative explains intended outcomes such as the determination of building compatibility throughout the city, achieving an understanding of community qualities, and the final assembly of area-by-area community-character manuals. Community photos were uploaded to the city's CodeNEXT Flickr account.[18]

As community members often relate to and listen more to their neighbors than professionals, encouragement toward useful group assembly of an urban diary–like product enables trust-building and community consensus. In each small group, people should be encouraged to discuss what they have photographed, which helps them to refine their ideas surrounding each photo and clarify expression.

The urban diary can also include community voice-sharing and perspectives, including classic tools such as photo-voice and image-preference surveys. In visual-preference surveys, the public ranks images of urban development or design in some way, based on what they like or dislike, or think is appropriate or inappropriate for their area. These surveys typically rely on images generated by the project team, not by the community. Community Image Survey, developed by the Center for Livable Communities, similarly shows contrasting slides from a local area. Survey managers then analyze results and calculate a numerical score for each image in order to establish consensus on preferred development or design outcomes.[19]

While these approaches seek public involvement in placemaking, they lack active immersion of the visual sense. If participants respond only to limited, professionally generated multiple-choice questions and photographs, the responses may fall short of outcomes from fuller participation. If community members submit photographs, decision-makers may be better informed as to preferred places in a neighborhood, or places that should be targeted for improvement. Community-generated photographs better allow for integrating what people like or dislike, reflecting emotions stirred by specific places.

As noted throughout this book, using photographs captured by professionals, who often don't live in the communities they are photographing, limits other perspectives from within the community, and may even create biases toward places arising from a photographer's gender, cultural background, and political agendas. The use of third-party photographers also undermines the sensory experiences of taking the photos, and the personal experience of seeing the surrounding areas.

Example: Crowd-Sourcing through Photovoice
(Yesler Terrace, Seattle)
Photovoice is a form of consultation in which cameras (generally disposable) are given to generally younger community members to "identify, record, represent, and enhance their community through specific photographic technique."[20] It is a technique designed to help residents tell their stories, prioritize issues, and inform decision-makers about issues or concerns, or successes and assets. The method can inform policy making while also providing visual evidence or input into issues, which allows for community expression, discussion, and sharing. Such initiatives endeavor to connect residents of changing neighborhoods to each other, enabling dialogue, shared voices, and potential lessons learned.[21]

A prototypical photovoice exercise recently took place at Seattle's Yesler Terrace, the first racially integrated public housing in the United States, dating from 1941. In 2012, the Seattle Housing Authority commenced a fifteen-year redevelopment of the neighborhood, from 500 townhouse-style buildings with over 1,200 ethnically diverse residents to high-rise housing and commercial space that will ultimately accommodate 30,000 people at completion. Many original residents have been relocated, potentially subjecting them to feelings of alienation and sudden disconnection.

Spurred by the redevelopment, a consortium of Seattle University and local media and youth–based organizations co-led a group of teenagers in the Yesler Terrace Youth Media Project in a standard photovoice exercise.[22] Over a seven-week summer program for multiple years, the students addressed several topics concerning the housing project and became *de facto* advocates for their community through documentary photography and video.[23]

One participant highlighted the loss of private gardens through the redevelopment to be a real concern for many residents. As noted by Debra Webb, "As a result of the compelling photographs and videos produced by the youth, Seattle Housing Authority executives and Seattle civic leaders now have an honest and unedited critique of the redevelopment efforts."[24] The Yesler Terrace approach shows how giving the public an opportunity to portray the status quo visually and voice their concerns about future development can better highlight community perspectives in decision-making processes and create dialogues with often overlooked voices. As one participant stated: "I know that I have a voice and I've learned that this community will face a lot of big changes because of the redevelopment. This makes me want to share my opinions and let people hear from a youth's perspective. There needs to be a change in voice."[25]

Urban diaries have great potential for assisting city authorities to refine project themes, possible processes, and forums, or to supplement the democratic design movement led by Detroit planning director Maurice Cox and others. Ultimately, in the spirit of Kushner's celebration of social media users as effective co-designers of today's architecture via immediate feedback loops, urban diaries have the potential to enable residents to co-design with city authorities, developers, and other players. Elicitation of community knowledge, with input from shared observations, creates greater potential for community members to feel sufficient degrees of ownership and engage as co-designers in the redevelopment context.

OTHER SMART-CITY EXAMPLES USING PHOTOGRAPHY

Three examples below show how photography is aggregated and used as data to inform municipal decisions and general conclusions about cities. The first "smart-city" example actually doubles as a community education / knowledge-seeking project as described above, while a second extends the use of "find it, fix it" data gathered by previously described reporting apps and platforms. Finally, a third example describes the use of data mining from photographs submitted to social media networks and other applications.

Understanding Flood Risks: California King Tides

Urban diary inputs can successfully be integrated with planning projects, as well as the evaluation of existing conditions or implementation of plans. These data inputs can be useful for creating documentary evidence of a neighborhood or city that is suitable for comparison after changes occur in the built environment. The California King Tides project invites members of the public to help understand flood risks and future sea-level rise in the Bay Area by sharing the photographs they've taken at high tide.[26] These participatory projects not only raise awareness of a planning issue but also enhance the "science" of urban-planning projects: a creative venture, photography provides objective data inputs that inform decision-makers.

Gauging Infrastructure: WalkScope

The presentation of such participatory "urban diary" projects through social media (often including photographs) can be used as a means of collecting numerical data that can also be used to evaluate a project's success. In Denver, WalkScope invites "find it, fix it" submittals on sidewalk quality, obstructions, safety issues, amenities, and other elements of walkable environments, and then collates data and presents results through graphs and maps.[27] In New York City, developer Dan Biederman uses the number of Bryant Park photo tags on Flickr and Twitter to gauge public opinion regarding the park.[28]

Data Mining from Photographs: Jetpac, Google Photos, and Airtick

More-subjective urban diary photographs are beginning to inform the more objective, data-based smart city. While city authorities are experimenting with how to interpret the value of photography for improving urban outcomes, technologies are emerging to remotely derive information from people's pictures. In 2014, Google purchased Jetpac, a city guides company that offers users advice on places to visit.[29] Jetpac uses image recognition and neural network technology to analyze billions of publicly shared photos on apps like Flickr and Instagram to determine happy and popular places. Jetpac developers contend that Jetpac's algorithms can mirror the way the brain learns to recognize elements in pictures or text.

In 2014, Jetpac identified Belfast as the United Kingdom's happiest city, based on its analysis of public Instagram photos.[30] The software analyzed 100 million location-tagged public photos on Instagram, with emphasis on people's facial expressions, colors, and objects. Jetpac technology assessed whether people in the photos were wearing lipstick (as an indicator of being dressed up to have a good time), and whether they had moustaches (as an indicator of the concentration of "hipsters").

While this study reflects some seemingly comical and lighthearted assumptions about indicators of people's happiness in cities, it highlights the potential for technology to evaluate the layers of meaning embedded in the billion photos taken worldwide each day (with 55 million shared on Instagram, and 5 million made public and then geotagged). According to the co-founder of Jetpac, Paul Warden, popular places get represented in hundreds or even thousands of photos. These pictures can then be analyzed by using new categories of people-generated "data exhaust" (the data generated as a by-product of people's online actions and choices) as fodder for more learning about our connections to, and experiences of, places.[31]

Google Photos, launched in 2015, is also likely to evolve as a pioneering technology that analyzes information from what the camera captures. In 2016, Apple followed suit with "advanced computer vision technology" that also offers sophisticated analysis and sorting of photographs. Although I cautioned earlier about the indiscriminate use of virtual photography as a substitute for in-person visits, the data-mining approach discussed here offers potentially exciting roles for urban diaries in helping both citizens and decision-makers to distill the necessary elements of the better city and to empirically test the foundational thinking of Kevin Lynch, Jane Jacobs, and others described throughout this book.[32]

Scientists are also starting to review and analyze individual photos in aggregated form, with the goal of enhancing livability by better understanding conditions and environmental qualities at certain locations, such as weather patterns, air quality, neighborhood dynamics, and social inequality.[33] AirTick, an app in development by researchers at Nanyang Technological University, uses crowd-sourced photos to analyze the haziness of the environment—a low-cost way to monitor air pollution.[34] AirTick will initially compare images to official air-quality data, and after extensive, image-based "learning" it will eventually be used to predict pollution levels by reading images. Based entirely on crowd-sourced photos, the app is ultimately designed to provide the public with real-time air pollution readings and related details such as the direction, duration, and intensity of sunlight. Such information will also help urban planners investigate opportunities to install solar panels.

In sum, our photographs, whether individual or crowd-sourced, highlight the features of the built and natural environment, as well as the ways that we interact with cities. Sharing photos through apps and social media platforms promotes both multiple and unique points of view, and spreads stories about people's experiences of their city. These stories unlock the city to new explorers and facilitate conversations about the city. With an estimated 2–3 trillion photos uploaded to the internet in 2015 alone, digital media also offers a significant research tool with a wealth of information supplied by shared photos. The smart city, or "internet of things," has yet to document fully our relationships with our cities and our visions of how to improve them.

Photography Platforms and the Bigger Picture

Cities often use photography platforms to seek general input or supplement planning efforts. The examples below show both general submittal approaches and a variety of participatory planning efforts that use submitted photographs to varying degrees, including distinct urban diary approaches.

GENERAL PLATFORMS AND BIG-PICTURE PLANNING SUPPLEMENTS

In addition to the innovation discussed so far, cities and projects often maintain an online platform or portal to allow submission of data, narratives, photographs, or, hypothetically, a full-fledged urban diary. This platform is often as simple as a social media account like Instagram, Flickr, Twitter, or Facebook, and sometimes a separate website. On such sites, people are often asked to participate in a "Photo Friday"–type event, such as the Seattle waterfront redevelopment and planning example recapped in chapter 2. As in the Vancouver example, cities often ask for photos that the submitter may like or dislike, or photos that show aspects of the city that the submitter would like to see more of, and cities also sometimes request documented examples from elsewhere (beyond the neighborhood or city or country).

Other photo requests tend to occur during longer-term, higher-level vision plans, such as a thirty-year plan which will then guide other, more-applied projects (e.g., Austin's CodeNEXT character studies and regulatory update) or a long-term approach to particular distinct urban areas. More recently, as suggested by the Melbourne example that follows, urban forest strategies increasingly include requests for photo documentation of tangible assets subject to inventory, such as notable neighborhood trees. An urban diary approach could provide a method for drawing attention to the importance of urban vegetation and tree canopies. Several cities have already begun to implement these methods and develop them into a more applied, Austin-like prototype.

USE OF URBAN DIARY APPROACHES AS PART OF LONG-TERM VISION / PLANS

Six examples from Canada, Australia, and the United States appear below. Collectively, these examples show a range of approaches to the use of photography in the long-term planning process, from elicited photography to a discrete urban diary component.

1. Abbotsford, British Columbia—Abbotsforward

In Abbotsford, British Columbia, Canada, the 2014 update to the Official Community Plan, Abbotsforward (one of the city's most valuable tools for guiding the way the community grows and develops), encouraged resident engagement by eliciting participation in the related "Picturing Your City" photo activity.[35] Residents were invited to send in pictures of places they like and dislike in Abbotsford, as well as places that do not exist in the city but should (termed "wishes"). The city used Twitter to spread the word about Picturing Your City. This approach helped to raise awareness and information about the project, as well as provide a conversation starter for receiving input.

The eighteen-month project officially launched in 2014 during Canada Day celebrations, with opportunities for residents to give their input regarding how Abbotsford will grow and develop over the coming years. The city received ninety-five photo submissions, categorized into "likes" and "dislikes" in an available report.[36] The city then proceeded to other engagement steps such as "citizen circles," community walks, and guest speakers, all to provide further input.

The Official Community Plan (OCP) provides guidance about future development; locations of parks and trails; different housing densities; public transit; and commercial, industrial, and agricultural development. The city's report on the photo submissions notes that the photos provided by the community could also be used in further stages of the project to illustrate themes, concepts, and new planning ideas.

This prospect, in the spirit of Picture Adelaide 2040 (discussed next), shows particular benefits of the urban diary approach. First, community-based photographs can obviate the need to direct a portion of the municipal budget to professional photographers. Second, as in Austin, citizens may be more apt to have a sense of ownership in planning reports that authentically reflect the community and their input through imagery.

2. Adelaide, South Australia — Picture Adelaide 2040

The city of Adelaide, South Australia, presents another instance in which an urban diary approach incorporates individual observational inputs as an associated component of a long-term planning or policy-making process. In fact, Adelaide made personal storytelling and observation a critical element of planning the city's future. Stage 1 of Adelaide's well-presented "Picture Adelaide 2040" project centered on gathering 1,000 stories from citizens (each with a photo) on how they use their favorite urban places.[37] Picture Adelaide 2040 was purposefully designed to collect photographs and stories to integrate and inform the development of several major plans: the Adelaide 2040 Plan, Strategic Plan 2016–2020, the Park Lands Strategy, District Planning, and the City of Adelaide Planning Strategy.

The Adelaide process was summarized in a 2015 report as a "'broad-based engagement' with the people who live, work, visit, or study in the city."[38] An advisory committee and city staff developed common themes from the Picture Adelaide stories and photos to inform ongoing planning, a process that continues today. The report repeatedly emphasizes the significant relationship between the collected stories and photographs and the development of planning goals and objectives, a clear reminder of the need to better wed the subjective soft city with the city of decision-makers.

3. Albany, New York—Albany 2030

Albany 2030: The City of Albany Comprehensive Plan, adopted in 2012, is the first comprehensive plan in the city's 400-year history. Albany 2030: Your City, Your Future is a framework for the city informed by research and community input, intended to guide (re)development and (re)investment to meet community needs.[39] As part of this project, Albany 2030 launched an interactive website to provide a comprehensive resource for outreach, feedback, and information sharing. A component of the "Share" section of the website includes a Citizen Journal, which allowed users to upload photos, text, and videos "describing opinions about Albany, strengths and challenges, and examples of what they envision for the future." Users can also participate in online surveys.

The project team also hosted several "Walk-shops," interactive walking tours to highlight plan themes and inform participants of related projects. Participants were invited to take photos of things they would like to see more of, as well as elements of the city they would like fixed or changed. At the meeting location, they were given the opportunity to share the ideas they captured during the walk. Two hundred photos were uploaded to Flickr, enabling the opportunity for others to view and comment on others' photos.

4. San Jose, California—Envision San Jose 2040

In 2009, the city of San Jose utilized photo-sharing as a component of its user-input-oriented, web-based wiki Envision 2040 process. The project sought resident input to guide city officials in the development of the Envision San Jose 2040 Plan. In concert with a nineteen-question survey, residents were asked to submit photographs depicting both San Jose's assets and its challenges, although people also posted photos of other places with elements they thought should be emulated.

Residents posted 129 photos on the Wikiplanning website. The pictures addressed a wide variety of topics, including but not limited to public art, bicycle lanes/facilities, farmers' markets, green roofs, parks, public spaces, parking lots, and urban form (including several photos referencing the number of stories on buildings, residential density, and architecture). Wikiplanning staff screened and posted all photos submitted by participants. Most of the pictures elicited at least some comments from other viewers, and these were also included in the report.[40]

5. Redmond, Washington — Old Town Historic Core Walk & Talk & Nuts & Bolts Workbook / Urban Diary

The city of Redmond, Washington, is a working laboratory addressing the human capacity to see and reflect on market-driven realities and the diversity of the stakeholders involved in most land-use matters. Redmond, in conjunction with Feet First, a pedestrian advocacy group, organized a walking tour and workbook explicitly designed for use by participants as an "urban diary." The tour was intended as a way for community members to consider the character and the built environment of the city's Historic Core, an important consideration for the city in light of pending civic infrastructure enhancements, ongoing development projects, and anticipated comprehensive plan and zoning amendments.

The city first analyzed methods of enhanced public outreach to facilitate its preservation planning goals, and then adopted an innovative and interactive outreach approach that included involvement of the public sector (the city administration), the nonprofit sector (FeetFirst), and the private sector (OneRedmond, a city-based business, technology, and economic development partnership). A city intern conducted an initial literature search that (1) examined prior inquiry (by scholars including Kevin Lynch, Jane Jacobs, and others) into how community character and sense of place are defined by layered, historic continuity (similar to the "age value" concept mentioned in chapter 4), and (2) examined public engagement methodology. The result was the integrated "Walk & Talk & Nuts & Bolts" program.

"Walk & Talk" events were a FeetFirst tradition in Washington State, aimed to promote walkable places, and the accessibility and safety associated with such places. Redmond staff added use of the urban diary tool, "a concept manifested by Chuck Wolfe in his theory of 'Urbanism Without Effort,' which stresses the power of urban observation in experiencing urban environments . . . [and] actively engaging with a place."[41] Significantly, summaries of the approach described the Redmond event as blending "the experiences of walking, talking, observing, and recording in a new and interactive way" by assimilating a two-part approach.[42] First, in a community meeting, planners discussed pending redevelopment in and around the Historic Core, and second, they led a combined walk and urban diary workbook exercise.[43]

The workbook provides a map of the Historic Core, featuring eleven stops.[44] The workbook is "pre-illustrated" by two photographs and followed by a series of focused questions about the Core's built and open-space environments, followed by several blank lines for participant answers. Questions focused on various features at each stop, such as pavement, vegetation, desired features for a future plaza, architectural elements, streetscape features, relationships among buildings and parking and storage, park-design elements, landscaping, facade preservation and enhancement, prospective park gateway features, types of walking surfaces, and potential alley improvements.

Subsequently, the workshop's final product consisted of collated, itemized summaries and preliminary analyses of the urban diary responses for each stop (including parklet and alley improvements, vegetation, connection to parks, wayfinding, activated street life and sidewalk width, consistency with local architecture, and building materials). The city staff then presented the summaries to the city's planning commission in concert with a range of architectural responses to show prospective outcomes for the Historic Core. The staff also proposed design standards based on intent statements, specific options dependent on location within the Core, visual guidance, and concept review. According to Senior Planner Kim Dietz and other project stakeholders, draft zoning-overlay provisions (based on the diary findings as adapted by staff and urban design professionals) were initially deemed problematic by certain property owners—particularly due to potential building facade materials and revised height limits—and the city delayed the original timeline and approach in order to reflect how best to address this response.[45]

Redmond's next step involves approaching stakeholders with alternative concepts for redevelopment in and around historic structures and asking stakeholders to provide their own alternatives for any redevelopment plans. In addition, the staff continues to work on proposed

Figure 5.4   The Redmond palette.

amendments to its overlay-zoning district and on working to incorporate a historic-preservation element into the city's Comprehensive Plan.[46]

Redmond may present the most advanced and well-considered application of the urban diary concept to date. The term *urban diary* is used explicitly, and the workshop expressly adopted the principles of my earlier book and articles. The Redmond experience also shows what happens when citizen input, based on visual clues, merges with a traditional land-use process and design regulations that affect individual property owners and, perhaps, property value.

The Redmond approach did not involve participant photography as a central element. Photographs and questions were preselected as cues by city staff and student interns for a single-instance event. Municipalities entertaining the use of urban diaries should consider the implications of the Redmond approach versus a more individually expressed photographic (or another form of expressed observation) facilitation. Would multiple approaches to photographing the eleven stops on the workshop guide map have altered the consensus around any issue, or would different perspectives have added even more complexity?

6. Melbourne, Australia—Long-Term Urban Forest Strategy
The city of Melbourne's Urban Forest Strategy used photography as a tool for consultation, and participants contributed specific responses to supplied photographs at a 2013 community workshop about long-term Central City greening plans. Though the photos were not termed an "urban diary," attendees at different tables were asked to view a pre-selected set of the same photographs depicting participants' desires for future greening, and then divide the photos into three character groups: "best represent the future Central City," "represent the future you don't want," and "photos you are unsure about or cannot agree upon." They were also asked to add a word or phrase to describe the grouped photos. A report summarized the groupings and ranked the descriptive words (e.g., "shady," "canopy," "diversity," "variety," "green," "avenue," "colour," "space for people").[47] Web portals also allowed crowd-mapping of individual locations with indications of "favourite trees" and suggestions for greening or increasing the number of trees.

This use of photography as input in the long-term urban forestry-planning context borrows from many approaches described earlier, and, as in Redmond, raises the issue of how individual photo submittals might change outcomes compared with results obtained from the use of photo cues. Melbourne's approach, involving both the natural and built environments, also highlights the potential role of other urban diary media. Over and above pictures and words, the sounds of birds and the wind in the leaves and perhaps even smells may be especially relevant to participants' points of view.

Illustrating the Patterns, Projects, and Players

This chapter has presented a diverse range of examples showing cities how to capitalize on social media in order to encourage residents to informally discover their city, or to generate enthusiasm around a city project or proposal. We have also noted a handful of examples in which cities make use of urban diary–like approaches to inform policy or planning outcomes, and we've seen how approaches that welcome photographic input tend to be part of longer-term visions or neighborhood-character projects. Initiatives that integrate photography into discussions around the use, experience, and development of city spaces are generally led by city governments, although several examples also highlight the use of photography by community groups to advocate for preferred outcomes. The remainder of chapter 5 attempts to summarize lessons learned regarding the affected stakeholders in most cities today, including residents, developers, and decision-makers.

SUMMARY TOOLKIT

The points below recap the significant opportunity for the urban diary to be a more mainstream component of urban-planning participation processes. There are many potential approaches for cities to explore, ranging from simple to more invested, including:

- Inviting residents to share their photographs of their local communities on social media and to provide formal input into a development proposal or planning project, in order to complement more traditional approaches. (Some considerations include the value of participant empowerment, "ownership," and "buy-in.")
- Mapping platforms that allow residents to contribute exemplary images to illustrate their commentary in response to a range of planning projects or initiatives. Such platforms have the potential for greater transparency, for people to understand each other's perspectives, and potentially for allowing people to vote on one another's feedback.
- Inviting residents to contribute urban diary–type submittals to assist with expanding knowledge about a particular issue and to complement technical inputs.

URBAN DIARIES AND THE DEVELOPER

Both institutional and small-scale developers seek certainty for their proposals in order to better assure the accuracy of pro forma spreadsheets or financial planning, site acquisition, design, site planning, and construction. To attract capital from banks or equity partners, they need a credible portrayal of feasibility, a realistic sense of timing, and an understanding of how future income streams from proposed uses will allow for debt service and income to offset development costs.

At the same time, bolder or more-extensive alterations to the urban landscape are often controversial among city residents and neighbors, and can require extensive local, state, and federal permitting, which adds time and expense. Governmental permitting processes create the opportunity for input through both conventional testimony and the sorts of innovations discussed in this and earlier chapters.

Murphy McCullough, the developer and former design review board chair mentioned in the introduction, maintains that, whenever possible, a collaborative discussion can steer the development process toward greater certainty through up-front discussion of visual and emotional factors that surround any project proposal.[48] Interviews conducted as research for *Seeing the Better City* confirmed that certain developers and their design and community-outreach teams know the value of advance public consultation. Open houses and focus groups, even before property purchase, can lead to less confrontational permitting scenarios, especially if affordability, business disruption, or "gentrification" is on the minds of community members.[49]

While serving as a land-use or environmental lawyer, I have been involved in several projects in which the developer has led community meetings outside of public process—ranging from brownfield development of empty urban parcels to professional sports facilities to affordable-housing opportunities—to elicit responses to a variety of prospective approaches or designs. These meetings, sometimes presented in charrette (stakeholder interactive design or input session) format, offer opportunities that are similar to government-led input sessions under local zoning and environmental review provisions. Sometimes, these privately sourced sessions can be combined with, or substituted for, legally mandated procedures.

Depending on the approach of a project team, privately sourced sessions often feature simulations of design alternatives or some form of augmented reality. One tool, produced by Seattle-based DRiVEdecisions, using publicly available data to create three-dimensional imagery of a development site or a neighborhood, contains multiple data overlays with infrastructure and market information and attempts to provide a visual understanding of developmental impact based on user manipulation of chosen scenarios.[50] Tools such as DRiVE show a further evolution of the community-involvement strategies described above and, although centered on simulations of future virtual views, could add an as-yet-untapped element to urban diary exercises. The urban diary approach has great potential for showing developers what the community desires for a particular area; why not also use augmented future three-dimensional simulations based on crowd-sourced visual information initially generated by a government?

The urban diary approach also translates well as a means for developers to disarm opposition and embrace local input, consistent with the personal approach urged by Marc Kushner. Using the elicited and contributed photography approaches discussed in this chapter, participants in a community meeting could work with and respond to photographs of the general area as well as examples from afar. Participants could also walk a site in a cooperative fashion and contribute to an information base about site history, community desires, and appropriate development types. Implementation of these simple steps may assure that a developer will gain a more immediate understanding of local desires.

Over the past several years, I have seen this approach followed as part of a developer's outreach for redevelopment of the four corners of a central-city intersection in Seattle. He used various elicited input, including a web page, while attempting to marshal a sense of appropriateness for his plans. Subsequently, however, the recession short-circuited both the development and outreach efforts, and development became more market-driven around apartments and some level of mixed-use development, even including two marijuana dispensaries. Arguably, robust local input suffered as a result of the more market-driven approach.

I am not suggesting that all design efforts should be pluralistic, that a site owner or developer should cede control to unlimited, widespread debate about how to proceed, or that the market will not play a significant role as to the sort of redevelopment that occurs. Rather, I would argue that, similar to a response to architectural style, the cycles of acceptance and disapproval of particular development approaches have rapidly evolved in the age of digital apps and media to broaden audiences and provide a capacity for immediate feedback. With the advent of smartphones and apps such as Instagram, we are all now architectural photographers and critics, and the prospect of immediate social media feedback should be both anticipated and, to some degree, championed by project proponents.

An urban diary approach could involve floating different development scenarios and allowing interested neighborhood urban diarists to supplement or complete design elements. The goal of embracing the urban diary tool could be not only to allow for the universal capacity of the city dweller to see and respond to the changing city, but also to avoid surprises in how a project evolves. If regular images of prospective projects were to appear on Instagram, Facebook, and similar platforms, then the end user will be able to experience several virtual visits prior to actual construction. The as-built project will be both collaborative and "already familiar" by the date of construction.

The urban diary also provides a significant opportunity to extend market research by making greater use of place-based information generated by the public. Such information can assist developers and designers in gaining a more significant impression of what is working, what is needed, or what is wanted by the local community, rather than leaving this to the developer's or city's sole discretion. Such an approach may also help developers and city decision-makers to understand better what the local community considers as appropriate or inappropriate development, thereby minimizing potential objections and controversies, and assisting politicians to know their constituents and the opportunities that they are seeking for their area.

Increasingly, developers of new residential buildings create unique marketing strategies to highlight the attributes of a local area—the quality of life and amenities on offer. These strategies may highlight the metrics of Walkscore or, more traditionally, the proximity to important streets, parks, or schools. But there is potential for developers to tap into the expertise of the existing community to assist with highlighting these qualities by fostering the production and discussion of urban diaries by residents, which may have the effect of strengthening local identity and community connections.

DESIGN, DIARIES, AND DEMOCRACY

Citizens who react to land-use decisions that affect them may benefit the most from urban diaries, because the urban diary is, at its core, a tool of empowerment and expression. Many of the approaches already suggested in chapters 3 and 4 and in this chapter define how city dwellers can inform both developers and governmental decision-makers about their preferences and, by doing so, gain a sense of ownership, participation, and belonging in how the spaces around them will change. Randolph Hester's extensive writings on ecological democracy are consistent with the goals and solutions set out here, in that urban diaries and the fruits of urban observation are intended to draw out basic human responses of satisfaction and comfort: "Ecological democracy will produce radically new forms of habitation, not in extravagant architecture but rather in a search for roots, foundations, and fundamentals—the basis of a satisfying life."[51]

To Hester, the form of the better city is one that fosters places where people and landscape can connect, cultural traditions will be honored, and community activities will thrive, none of which need definition by architecture. Hester speaks with carefully chosen language, stressing the landscape, sacredness, and sustainability; he examines, for instance, how to make density attractive based on interaction with green space, allowing for privacy, and incorporating public transit access. I mention Hester here because his approach to describing urban form centers on the core values of the city dweller, and he encourages approaches that will resonate and enable, an approach followed by the Redmond staff.

Hester also provides a holistic approach to design theory attempting to capture the real mixture of the visionary and the practical that I suggest people explore through urban diaries, and he examines the type of considerations often lacking in the planning, policy, and regulatory arenas. His focus on our core values allows for thoughtful expression through urban diaries, including photographs, about what works for each of us: "For those of us who make cities, theory takes shape from intellectual inquiry and experience. We learn from success and failure. Why did this work and that fail? If something works, we keep doing it and it becomes a thesis. If it fails, we ponder it. Design theory often adjusts to realities of implementation until that theory is meaningful."[52]

Urban diaries can be a way for those affected by land-use decisions to state, early on, what their preferences are in a fashion that says more than just "no." Too often, project proponents are stymied by individuals or groups who intend simply to stop or delay a project, policy, or regulatory amendment rather than to provide meaningful input about what resonates for them.

I don't think this is a naïve proposition, but I do admit that this approach assumes collaboration, as attempted in Redmond, and will not work where parties are at odds with one another and are unwilling to consider each other's point of view. It will not work for every plan that assumes more density in a neighborhood, or that proposes a new building with contrasting style and scale next door. But an urban diary, as noted, can empower, provide context, and provide a more concrete basis for melding different points of view. If a charrette or mediation can succeed where contentious public hearings or legal proceedings would only cause delay and uncertainty, the increased use of the diary tool might see the light of day.

Informing Better Decisions

One way or another, a crowd-sourced approach, whether directed or generated from the grassroots, has increasing promise for informing better decisions. As summarized already, such approaches coalesce ideas, gather people together, and achieve a form of collective wisdom not otherwise available. Nevertheless, it's important to acknowledge that crowd-sourcing is still in its infancy, and issues of facilitation (i.e., the number of users) and credibility remain unresolved. Nonetheless, the visually illustrative aspects of crowd-sourcing offer great promise.[53]

Ryan Smolar, a reader of my earlier articles on the urban diary concept, frames the practical uses of urban diaries based on different conceptions of crowd-sourcing in an essay on "bottom-up" community participation strategies. Smolar comments on my past urban diaries "of various cities, a mix of broken staircases, repurposed plazas, street vendors, and smiling neighbors that inform the historic and human context of their environs in an obvious 'simple beauty.'" He provides a three-part analysis that is very helpful in framing the practical implications of *Seeing the Better City*.[54]

As I have advocated, Smolar suggests a "top-down" leadership role in which a leader provides an urban diary or encourages stakeholders to create or crowd-source urban diary examples, and he suggests further that this strategy could provide a satisfactory method for working with community leaders. He also proposes a bridge approach in which a journalist, another stakeholder, or a "random do-gooder" provides the "middle tissue" to align top-down and bottom-up perspectives. Finally, he advises: "So, my 'BOTTOM-UP' friends, if you find yourself railing against some senseless [proposal] (from your well-informed perspective), don't go at them with the fury, but with a handful of photos illustrating the true urban form—the issue and/or the bright spot solution created by natural human ingenuity. If you can't produce such a resource, petition to have one created by those mentioned above."[55]

Among the simplest "crowd-sourced" urban diaries is a set of observations sent by e-mail or social media, showing a problem worthy of correction, or an idea, or a statement, whether pro or con. Former Seattle council member Sally Clark underscored how she and her staff reviewed and responded to these communications when I asked about the public-input experience she garnered while chairing the council's land-use committee.[56] As also noted throughout this book, appended photographs (either as e-mail attachments or embedded into posts on Facebook, Instagram, Flickr, Twitter, Google+, Pinterest, or Tumblr) enhances verbal commentary or allows the image to become the statement in itself. Elected officials, as well as public outreach for projects, should always allow for photo submittal as a form of citizen participation.

One natural input for urban diaries is to include them as part of evolving regulatory approaches that already call for the content that urban diaries can offer. We have identified participatory mapping approaches that inform crowd-sourced conclusions about special places, as well as other forms of elicited photography, whether academic or professionally based. A similar opportunity for input comes from participatory approaches to regulatory revision or design input.

The charrette setting is often an opportunity for a "crowd" of community members to supply information on the merits or perceived detriments of a new project or proposed regulation, and to submit perceptions of the existing conditions of a surrounding area. Form-based codes, and some area-wide design guidelines, for instance, redefine the focus of development regulations as forms of buildings and streets and uniform physical characteristics, rather than the type of land use. These code approaches require an initial characterization of existing building typologies and the "look and feel" of the candidate area. Such early characterizations, often conducted in charrettes, could incorporate the use of photo-centric urban diaries to catalog existing building forms.

To guide permit application submittals, progressive cities now commonly use Flickr to show photographs of how design guidelines might apply to building appearance, site relationships, access, and exemplary projects.[57] Flickr examples provide a threshold for the use of the urban diary to supplement existing process. A photo-centric urban diary could help document and answer common questions about typologies that already exist, and whether community support exists for their replication.

Similarly, in jurisdictions with design review processes (whether conducted by staff, an existing regulatory body, or a separate board or commission), submittal of urban diaries for consideration could assist decision-makers during early design guidance or full review and deliberation. Design review typically addresses such contextual aspects of a building or site as the following, used in the Seattle process:

1.   The overall appearance of the building.
2.   How the proposal relates to adjacent sites and the overall street frontage.
3.   How the proposal relates to unusual aspects of the site, like views or slopes.
4.   Pedestrian and vehicular access to the site.
5.   Quality of materials, open space, and landscaping.[58]

The design review process is often criticized as being infused with the subjectivity of the decision-makers, despite the application of "objective" standards or guidelines at the citywide or neighborhood-specific level. Applicants are often subject to the whims of neighbors opposed to a project's style, scale, or the proposed number or type of dwelling units. The same holds true for projects that comply with zoning requirements, particularly height and materials, but neighbors or retained professionals assert "incongruity," as discussed in chapter 4: they argue that a proposal is out of place with a neighborhood's preexisting character, with recognized historic districts, or with overlays— even when the proposed project may be answering a need for housing or other services in an urban sub-area.

In such cases, often centered in historic or "character" districts, debates tend to address "density versus preservation," incompatibility, scale, "overpowering" adjacent structures, and loss of neighborhood soul. These traditional urban squabbles could more purposefully include visual examples that support a varied interpretation of compatibility and scale requirements. Usually, only the proposed submittal by the developer advances arguments with visual examples. Even without a regulatory requirement to do so, a record could contain a far more extensive set of urban diaries, carefully prepared and subject to individual submittal requirements, presented by all participants in the review process or public hearings.

To that end, why not require a more systematic submittal by participants and commenters in which they chronicle their neighborhood and
state more concisely—and represent visually—the perceived shortcom-
ings of a proposal? Could such a requirement improve the process of
design review, meet the standards of case law that require more than
statements of subjective feelings by decision-makers, and take discussions
beyond mere oppositional tactics to a more meaningful deliberation?
Similar to the Redmond project and other planning or programmatic
walk projects, urban diaries could also complement site visits, where relevant, to document existing conditions and establish the positive and/or
negative impacts of proposed improvements or pending changes:

> *In addition to a site visit by _____, any member of the public with
> standing may submit an urban diary to document the perceived positive
> and/or negative impacts of _____. The urban diary may show similar
> projects and impacts from outside of the City, where relevant, and any
> such submittal shall explain and/or illustrate the basis for inclusion
> in the site visit record. Photographs used for the urban diary shall be
> labeled by location, and summarized by caption, and the identity of the
> photographer indicated on the lower left corner on the back of each such
> photograph.*

In legislative settings, campaigns often marshal support for new
policies and programs that may affect the look and feel of a city, ranging from affordable housing and transportation initiatives to new zoning provisions slated to expand development near transportation. Many
times, I have seen advocacy from a full range of business-based groups
or nonprofit environmental organizations supply form templates for
members or constituents to submit to the legislative body in support or
opposition of the matter at hand. Sometimes messages are combined
and streamlined by organizations working together in the form of a
"coalition letter." As a result, council members, legislators, and their
staffs receive multiple communications that are not at all customized. I
understand from knowledgeable sources that elected officials may take
note of the number received, but without much concern about original
letter content.

I suggest that, as with the record for a particular project application,
individual advocacy through urban diaries might be a more meaningful

form of public comment. Submittal of imagery that illustrates support or opposition could elevate the public dialogue and provide concrete points of view heretofore expressed only in words. While review might be more time consuming, the basis for decisions may prove more well informed, contributing to long-term positive impact.

As noted, photo-centric urban diaries could enhance the role that imagery already plays in the development of certain types of zoning regulations that concentrate on building form over the traditional emphasis on the uniform use of land by district. Some forms of regulation, such as form-based codes, or districting for historic structures, already rely on extensive documentation and inventorying of existing conditions. Parolek et al. have noted the role of stakeholder input to the consultant team in assembling existing development frameworks and building typologies, including "transect photo sheets," according to the Charrette Institute's Dynamic Planning process.[59]

In addition to the programmatic and toolkit examples described above, there are other opportunities for stakeholders to take a more central role in visioning processes whereby illustrative planning takes place to elicit and propose new forms of development to a community. City dwellers who have actively worked on their urban diaries would have a head start in public meetings and brainstorming sessions. The consultant team would be wise to solicit input with this approach in mind.

This method took place, at least in theory, in the reinventer.paris project, beginning in 2015, as a range of participants, including artists, were invited to join teams that would present ideas to address twenty-three available development sites around the city. Mayor Hidalgo's call for proposals addressed some of the same subjects addressed in *Seeing the Better City*:

A city like Paris must be able to reinvent itself at every moment in order to meet the many challenges facing it. Particularly in terms of housing and everything relating to density, desegregation, energy, and resilience. It is important in today's world to find new collective ways of working that will give shape to the future metropolis.

We are launching this call for innovative urban projects in order to prefigure what the Paris of tomorrow might be. Each

team is invited to present its ideas on how to bring added vitality
to exceptional Parisian sites. The winners will then be able to
purchase or rent the terrains in order to carry out their projects
while simultaneously conducting an urban experiment on an
unparalleled scale.[60]

The web-based "call for innovative projects" contained a meet-up page
that called for uploading suggestions (including visual) and participat-
ing in forming submittal teams.[61] The initial results were controversial,
however, partially because many selections did not meet the city's hope
for crowd-sourced teams comprised of more than each team's architect
and financier.[62]

These practical examples underscore the importance of understanding photographic methods, as outlined in chapter 3, by those ultimately
preparing land-use submittals. While smartphone photos are easily
generated, they will be weighed against more-professional exhibits prepared by project proponents, staff, or associated consultants. This is one
reason why careful attention to learning urban diary techniques may be
well warranted, and both government and private-sector entities may
consider workshops and seminars to communicate more formally the
principles presented in this book and toolkit summaries.

For actual permit submittals, the variation in land-use permitting
processes among different localities does not allow for a uniform recommended time for urban diaries to be added to a record. An urban
diary could be a component of a permit submittal through use of the
following or similar language:

*The applicant may submit testimony in the form of an urban diary to
supplement other materials. The urban diary may contain photographs
that document a project feature as it relates to the surrounding
vicinity, and that indicate how such feature will interact with existing
conditions and affect the experience of project users or passers-by. The
applicant shall indicate who prepared the urban diary and the included
photographs, the location portrayed, and the relevance of the photograph
to the proposal.*

On a larger scale, from the standpoint of decision-makers, a governmental decision-maker or decision-making body could establish a

"Big Idea" competition each year, and select the winning entry from the elicited urban diary submittals:

> *By January ___ of each year, the City of _____ shall establish a priority*
> *project to improve the quality of life for City residents. The ____*
> *shall, by September 1 of the preceding year, enumerate five alternative*
> *priorities and invite submittals by applicants. By November 1 of the*
> *previous year, applicants shall submit an urban diary that illustrates*
> *existing conditions and potential improvements relative to their chosen*
> *alternative. The potential improvements may be based on urban*
> *observation undertaken in the City, or elsewhere, including international*
> *venues. Each submittal must adapt examples to the context of the City,*
> *with specific attention to applicability under local conditions.*

Finally, another idea for incorporating urban diaries into the regulatory process might address the issues raised in my conversation with Lee Einsweiler, a main inspiration for this book, as well as formalize the Redmond approach documented above. Consider a code provision that allowed for an urban diary submittal to detail the public/private envelope left open for facade and streetscape treatment:

> *In the _____ overlay zone, facade design and interface with sidewalk*
> *and/or adjacent public rights-of-way will be approved based on review*
> *of an urban diary submittal. The urban diary, which may show*
> *solutions deemed relevant by the applicant, must contain a summary*
> *of why the demonstrated treatments are appropriate in the project and*
> *locational context, and how each feature complies with City standards*
> *for _____ and _____ under Section _____ of the Code.*

As emphasized throughout this chapter, converting idealistic notions of better cities to concrete, discernable, resilient places is no small matter, but the task is well under way. I have shared many examples of evolving ways of characterizing the urban environment, and how our individual expressions can address what the better city can be. It will be exciting to watch the evolution of infusing the human, equitable city into policy and regulatory processes through evocative photographs, using the urban diary, other toolkits, and other smart-city, "data-driven" approaches.

CONCLUSION

—

WHAT THE BETTER CITY CAN BE

Seeing the Better City provides multiple perspectives on how to organize and apply insights about urban space and envision sustainable places. Human relationships to cities and neighborhoods can be pursued as art, science, or a combination of both, as a source of academic study and as real-time experiences of professionals and residents.

Like my previous book, *Urbanism Without Effort*, the chapters presented here emphasize the visual sense and photography, and encourage city dwellers to look around and respond to what they see, regardless of how their responses are reviewed or processed for further use. Some readers may instinctively seek and see an order in physical surroundings. Others may see the irregular, organic city that has evolved over time. Either way, the most important outcome is that the reader learns the real value of speaking with more than words, and responds to places of physical order (like the Place des Vosges) aware of the vast range of forces that undergird their form and history.

Consequently, many sections of this book have addressed a better understanding of the underlying, fundamental relationships between people and cities, both by examining the emotion-based "soft city" from within and the externally viewed city form of buildings, streets, and other built-environment features. Through the urban diary in particular, I have outlined different ways to document emotional, observation-based perceptions from within and without, and to restate them in productive ways. I have been especially motivated to help find more ways for city officials to incorporate residents' personal exploration and observation into the more forward-looking tasks discussed in chapter 5.

Whether motivated by the *flâneur* precedent, perspectives on the evolved Paris of today, Jonathan Raban's words, or Berenice Abbott's photographs, my message to readers is simple. It is critically important for all of us, no matter what our backgrounds or inclination, to explore, observe, and share our observations in the interest of improving multiple aspects of the urban space around us. Our specific approaches may vary, but the concept of an immersive urban diary should guide the way, providing a versatile tool that can accommodate many techniques of observing and recording—anything from mental notes and remembered visions to written words and shared photographs.

I know from my recent experiences, whether in Paris, Fremantle, Perth, London, or beyond—let alone my much-cited hometown of Seattle—urban diaries are sources of personal inspiration, and when shared and contrasted, they reveal rich and instructive narratives, with often common themes. They show day-to-day motivations that we can marshal for use in urban policy, planning, and regulation, and as part of project advocacy and opposition.

The lessons of *Seeing the Better City* do not require a design education; a unique curriculum is not necessary to achieve a basic understanding of what visual and emotional factors may motivate a sense of a better place. In fact, one success of both the modern, less-formalistic placemaking movement and the "public life-study approach" may be their shared orientation around people and the human scale, and related tactical urbanism practices, rather than around rigid design criteria.

So what, in the end, *is* the better city, and how do we find it? Not, in my opinion, through blind acceptance of others' points of view, or through assumptions we have not ourselves explored. I think we find the better city straightforwardly, by looking and deciding on what inspires us. The good thing about a camera is that it often captures the "teaching moments" of inspiration, discussed earlier, for later reference and communication.

We may first instinctively see the better city in ordered architecture, or in a composition that emphasies a comfortable symmetry that organizes our understanding. I saw it recently in the auto-filled scene on this book's cover, with pedestrians crossing a wide avenue on a rainy day, with my eyes drawn to the people contrasting with the focal point in the distance, the monumental structure of the Paris Opera. But that doesn't mean that I support wide streets and automobile congestion in my city's future.

Rather, I prefer to think that it shows the value of deconstructing first impressions as a prelude to thoughtful deliberation about what the better city is. That is something that our inner critics can do, without being told what to think about what we see. In the instance described, it was the black-and-white convergence of the Avenue de L'Opéra upon the building itself, contrasting with the color of the pedestrians crossing in front—a nuanced juxtaposition of people, buildings, light, and scale.

Impressions like this one suggest that we should be careful in signing on to points of view that are absolute promoters or detractors of, say, tall residential buildings in an urban core. I have read—and mentioned here early on—articles that focus only on the evils of building height and luxury units, suggesting that their nature and form are purely market-driven. Under this analysis, the better city is something over which we have no control, as the real estate market will create the environment we see, no matter what we do.

To accept such an argument is to yield to a defeatist acceptance of others' characterizations of urban change, one that presumes, without reflection, absolute positives and negatives. As discussed earlier, while Berenice Abbott noted the role of photography in exposing planning failures, she also explained how certain tall buildings are easily cast as beautiful, ugly, or a mixture of both.

At this point in the concluding chapter, it is fair to ask: What is the ideal culmination of exploring, observing, and sharing in the urban environment? Other than going out and looking around, what can each of us, and our neighbors, do immediately to benefit from the many ideas discussed here and the many images displayed?

First, it is important once again to stress the role of the images presented here. By and large, they were meant to illustrate core messages behind what we see when we choose to look critically. Among those messages are the need to consider the naturally occurring, organic evolution that underlies planned development in cities; the multiple forces that shape the appearance of urban spaces; and the role of context in how ideas are applied—not to mention what directly resonates, both at first glance and on second look. Other considerations include the role of "pop-up" versus permanent uses, and an understanding that places survive differently (sometimes just as ideas without form).

Second, some would say these messages are just the "tip of the iceberg" in today's cities, and that no civic discussion should proceed without discussion of affordability, safety, and the quality of schools and transportation infrastructure. But simply seeing the multiplicity of issues that arise as part of the observations we make as we move from place to place is a start. Rather than resign ourselves to NIMBY-driven, protectionist discussion, perhaps if we can talk about what we see, it would elevate civic dialogue, premised on diary inputs—sense-based visual cues—prepared in anticipation of meaningful participation in a non-threatening environment.

Finally, now, to the immediate task, which I offer straightforwardly and without the structure of a complex study. Just seek out people who live nearby, and work with them to see the better city by exploring, observing, and speaking the visual language that you have read so much about here. My experience suggests that others will be equally inter-ested to share their personal cities and the juxtapositions that they, too, capture when they purposefully and critically explore.

My surmise is that if everyone would commit to listening and reflec-tion, people would feel both motivated and empowered to take some part of the experience to the next step. Someone would inevitably ask whom, in government, to talk to about, say, sidewalk maintenance or a height limit, or whether the shed across the street should have a permit. In fact, this could be a good juncture for inserting a new variable—a visitor could join in, or a city staff member, or an elected official, some-one who had also traveled the same or similar routes and recorded his or her response in an urban diary.

Given this approach, which attempts to honor human curiosity and the capacity to explore and observe, this "trickle-up" exercise could have a chance to improve the area under focus if it were later recognized as valid input by affected parties. This more spontaneous approach to urban diaries starts with casual inquiry and discussion rather than a formal input process, which could be a game-changer in empowering city dwellers to watch the world around them with a new point of view. At a minimum, such neighborly efforts, perhaps once more widespread (and reminiscent of the Austin CodeNEXT toolkit), should be added to the "elicited photography" approaches and facilitated diary-like efforts to shaping cities' futures. What would be better than self-realized responses to visual and sense-based prompts in advancing this book's purpose of promoting exploration, observation, and city improvement?

Whatever the observational tool employed, and however cities go about attempting to implement the best of what we see, some professionals today, who promote more pedestrian-friendly and sustainable approaches to design, often comment that the best practices that emerge from "seeing the better city" are now illegal under current codes. The enemy is usually the vast array of health and safety provisions that have developed in response to auto-centric places, focused on the demands and standards necessary for the ingress and egress of large vehicles.

As a lawyer who has more than once seen the street-width requirements of the fire marshal carry the day, I agree that accomplishing needed reform is often frustratingly slow. But, as a writer and photographer overseas, I have observed the best practices of the "better city" already implemented. Since 2009, I have tried to communicate these best practices visually so that others will not only hear words but see what they have not experienced themselves. Many such examples are contained in the urban diary excerpts throughout this book.

This is why more of us need to speak the language of our senses, even in more ideally subdued places such as City Hall, and in the meetings associated with urban development and change. Inevitably, whatever the cause—aging materials, impacts of nature, or changing technologies—things are going to look different with time. Consider, for instance, how urban space may be altered again with the dawn of the driverless car.

Seeing the Better City, as noted early on, is not about observation for observation's sake, but about applying positively the best of what we see. We have learned that the image-filled coffee-table book of old may also contain images for group discussion, project submittal, social media upload, or smart-city aggregation so that a remarkable, evocative view might also add an indicator of happiness, popularity, or air quality. When it comes to seeing the better city, the phrase "Let me show you what I mean" has never been more relevant, or more expansive. I hope that more of us will soon have images to share.

NOTES

All links verified as of August 2016.

Preface Notes

1. Jonathan Raban, *Soft City* (New York: E.P Dutton & Co., 1974), 2.
2. Peter Zumthor, "A Way of Looking at Things," *Thinking Architecture* (Basel: Birkheiser, 1998), 10.
3. Charles R. Wolfe, *Urbanism Without Effort* (Washington, DC: Island Press, 2013).
4. M. R. Wolfe, "A Visual Supplement to Urban Social Studies," *Journal of the American Institute of Planners* 31, no. 1 (February 1965), 51–62.
5. Ibid, 51.
6. Charles Baudelaire, "Le Cygne (The Swan)," in *Fleurs du mal* (1861), trans. Will Schmitz, http://fleursdumal.org /poem/220.
7. Timothy Egan, "Dude, Where's My City?" *New York Times*, April 1, 2016, http://www.nytimes.com/2016/04/01/opinion /dude-wheres-my-city.html.
8. Froma Harrop, "Don't Bury Our Cities in Megatowers," *Creators Syndicate*, February 25, 2016, https://www.creators .com/read/froma-harrop/02/16/dont-bury-our-cities-in -megatowers.

Introduction Notes

1. Lee Einsweiler, interview, April 2015.
2. Allowing regulatory flexibility within predefined areas is also a feature of "Lean Urbanism," a movement intended to foster creative, low-cost approaches to redevelopment, based on work funded by the Kresge Foundation.

3. For example, the *D.C. Retail* Tumblr blog provides extensive photographic evidence of former retail uses in residential areas of Washington, DC, to show neighbors the extent of former neighborhood businesses and help counter opposition to flexible mixed-use zoning.

4. Mike McGinn, interview, October 2015.

5. Allan Jacobs and Donald Appleyard, "Toward an Urban Design Manifesto," Working Paper, 1982, *Journal of the American Planning Association* 53, no. 1 (Winter 1987), 112–20.

6. Kevin Lynch and Malcolm Rivkin, "A Walk Around the Block," *Landscape* 8, no. 3 (Spring 1959), 24.

7. Jacques Yonnet, *Paris Noir: The Secret History of a City*, trans. Christine Donougher (London: Dedalus Books 2006), 1. Yonnet's task in *Paris Noir* was very different from my own, yet his focus on immersion shows, in human terms, how the more compellingly authentic aspects of city life emerge over time:

    You're no true Parisian, you do not know your city, if you haven't experienced its ghosts. To become imbued with shades of gray, to blend into the blind spots, to join the clammy crowd that emerges, or seeps, at certain times of day from the metros, railway stations, cinemas, and churches, to feel a silent and distant brotherhood with the lonely wanderer, the dreamer in his shy solitude, the crank, the beggar, even the drunk—all this entails a long and difficult apprenticeship, a knowledge of people and places that only years of patient observation can confer. (*Paris Noir*, 1)

8. Luc Sante, *The Other Paris* (New York: Farrar, Straus and Giroux, 2015), 25.

9. Murphy McCullough, interview, March 2016.

10. Michael Heater, "Making the Camera Your Friend," *Planning* 79, no. 8 (October 2013), 31.

11. Anne Whiston Spirn, *The Eye Is a Door* (Georgia, USA: Wolf Tree Press, 2014), 1–2, e-book available at: http://www.theeyeisadoor.com/#3.

12. Ibid., 2.

13. Randall Arendt, "The Highly Effective Planner," *Planning* 77, no. 5 (May/June 2011), 48.
14. Yi-Fu Tuan, *Topophilia* (Englewood Cliffs, NJ: Prentice-Hall, 1974).
15. Matthew Carmona, Steve Tiesdell, Tim Heath, and Tanner Oc, *Public Spaces—Urban Places* (Oxford, UK: The Architectural Press, 2010), 177; this book references fundamentals that are described in: Christopher Alexander, Sara Ishikawa, and Murray Silverstein, *A Pattern Language: Towns, Building, Construction* (Oxford, UK: Oxford Press 1977).
16. Nan Ellin, "The Tao of Urbanism," in *What We See: Advancing the Observations of Jane Jacobs*, ed. Stephen A. Goldsmith and Lynne Elizabeth (Oakland, CA: New Village Press, 2010), 44–56.
17. Nicole Brodeur, "'The Pretty and the Gritty': Tim Durkan Photographs Seattle's Forgotten," *Seattle Times*, March 18, 2016, http://www.seattletimes.com/seattle-news/the-pretty-and-the-gritty-tim-durkan-photographs-seattles-forgotten/.
18. The words cited here can be found in many quotation websites online, with attribution to Orson Welles. The passage appears to be abbreviated from a 1982 BBC interview (no longer available online) about Welles's career:

> I think it is very harmful to see movies for movie-makers because you either imitate them or worry about not imitating them. And you should do movies innocently. The way Adam named the animals the first day in the garden. And I lost my innocence. . . . I don't believe in learning from other people's pictures. I think you should learn from your own interior vision of things and discover, as I say, innocently, as though there had never been D. W. Griffith or Eisenstein or Ford or Renoir or anybody.

19. Allan Jacobs, "Looking at Cites," *Places Journal* 1, no. 4 (1984); the article discusses ideas from his book *Looking at Cities* (Cambridge, MA: Harvard University Press, 1985), 32.

20. See Charles Landry's website: http://charleslandry.com. As Landry wrote in "The City as a Lived Experience," in *Monocle* (July/August 2007): "The city is an assault on the senses. . . . Think of the smells, sounds, and visual battering. . . . The city is a lived experience. We feel it. It engenders emotions. It effects our psychology. We forget the smells, sounds, the touch, and even taste of the city and perhaps look without observing."

21. George Nelson, *How to See—A Guide to Reading Our Man-Made Environment* (Oakland, CA: Design Within Reach, 2003), xxi.

22. Gene Balk, "Teardown Town: 1,500 Small Houses Replaced by Giants since 2012," *Seattle Times*, November 27, 2015, http://www.seattletimes.com/seattle-news/data/teardown-town-1500-small-houses-replaced-by-giants-since-2012/.

23. Gene Balk, "Before-and-After Photos of Amazon's South Lake Union Turf," *Seattle Times*, January 19, 2016, http://www.seattletimes.com/seattle-news/data/amazons-south-lake-union-turf-do-you-recognize-this-place/.

24. J. B. Wogan, "How Mobile, Alabama, Used Instagram to Address Blight," *Governing*, November 20, 2015, http://www.governing.com/topics/transportation-infrastructure/gov-mobile-alabama-blight-instagram.html.

25. James Brasuell, Chris Steins, and Abhijeet Chavan, "Top 10 Websites—2015," *Planetizen*, January 6, 2016, http://www.planetizen.com/node/83095/top-10-websites-2015; see also: Jennifer Evans-Cowley, "The Best Planning Apps for 2016," *Planetizen*, January 4, 2016, http://www.planetizen.com/node/82996/best-planning-apps-2016.

26. See, for instance, the Slow Ottowa Pinterest board that portrays, among other things, exemplary complete streets, walkable paths, and bikeways: https://www.pinterest.com/slowottawa/.

27. Jennifer Evans-Cowley, "Time to Try Pokémon Go: Augmented Reality Connecting People to Places," *Planetizen*, July 13, 2016, http://www.planetizen.com/node/87335/time-try-pokémon-go-augmented-reality-connecting-people-places.

Chapter 1 Notes

1. Kevin Lynch, *The Image of the City* (Cambridge, MA: MIT Press, 1960), 3.
2. Mechelle Hankerson, "East Raleigh Residents Look for Alternative to City's Redevelopment Plan," *News & Observer* (Raleigh, NC), January 17, 2016, http://www.newsobserver .com/news/local/community/midtown-raleigh-news /article55199945.html.
3. Danny Westneat, "Get Rid of Single-Family Zoning? These Conversations Should Not Be Secret," *Seattle Times*, July 7, 2015, http://www.seattletimes.com/seattle-news/get-rid-of -single-family-zoning-in-seattle-housing-task-force-says-in -draft-report/.
4. *Seattle Times*, "City Needs to Slow Down and Make the Case on Housing Affordability Plan," July 16, 2015, http: //www.seattletimes.com/opinion/editorials/city-needs-to -slow-down-and-make-the-case-on-housing-affordability -plan/.
5. Charles R. Wolfe, *Urbanism Without Effort* (Washington, DC: Island Press, 2013).
6. Charles R. Wolfe, "Corners as the Baseline of Urbanism," *myurbanist* (blog), June 11, 2011, http://www.myurbanist .com/archives/6476; Charles R. Wolfe, "Why the 'Sit-able City' Is the Next Big Idea," *myurbanist* (blog), October 9, 2013, http://www.myurbanist.com/archives/9997.
7. Lloyd Alter, "Sit-able Cities Are as Important as Walkable Cities," *Treehugger*, October 17, 2013, http://www.treehugger .com/urban-design/sit-able-cities-are-important-walkable -cities.html; see also: William H. Whyte's work, *The Social Life of Small Urban Spaces* (Washington, DC: Conservation Foundation, 1980), carried on today by the Project for Public Spaces (http://www.pps.org/); see also: Jan Gehl and Birgitte Svarre, *How to Study Public Life* (Washington, DC: Island Press, 2013). Several other sources remind us of human "ecosystems," from Andrew L. Dannenberg, Howard Frumkin, and Richard J. Jackson, *Making Healthy Places: Designing and Building for Health, Well-being, and*

Sustainability (Washington, DC: Island Press, 2011), to concepts central to Kaid Benfield's collection of essays, *People Habitat: 25 Ways to Think about Greener, Healthier Cities* (Washington, DC: People Habitat Communications and Island Press, 2014).

8. Gehl and Svarre, *How to Study Public Life*, 3.

9. Jane Jacobs, *The Death and Life of Great American Cities* (New York: Random House, 1961).

10. Ibid., ix.

11. Walter Benjamin, "Paris, the City in the Mirror: Declarations of Love by Poets and Artists to the 'Capital of the World,'" in *On Photography*, ed. and trans. Esther Leslie (London: Reaktion Books, 2015), 358–59.

12. Joseph Rykwert, *The Seduction of Place: The History and Future of Cities* (New York: Vintage Books, 2002).

13. Jonathan Raban, *Soft City* (London: Harvill Press, 1974).

14. J. B. Jackson, "The Discovery of the Street," in *The Necessity for Ruins, and Other Topics* (Amherst, MA: University of Massachusetts Press, 1980).

15. Roger Cohen, "France Decapitated," *New York Times*, July 9, 2014, http://www.nytimes.com/2014/07/09/opinion/roger -cohen-france-decapitated.html?_r=0.

16. See: Grant McCracken, "Morgan Friedman, Turning Flaneurs into Planners," *CultureBy*, September 17, 2008, http: //cultureby.com/2008/09/morgan-friedman.html.

Chapter 2 Notes

1. Grady Clay, *Close-Up: How to Read the American City* (Chicago: University of Chicago Press, 1980), 11.

2. Tony Hiss, *The Experience of Place* (New York: Vintage Books, 1991).

3. See: Ann Sussman and Justin B. Hollander, *Cognitive Architecture—Designing How We Respond to the Built Environment* (New York: Routledge, 2015).

4. Charles Montgomery, *Happy City: Transforming Our Lives Through Urban Design* (New York: Farrar, Straus, and Giroux, 2013).

5. I have argued many times that close examination of past livability depicted in historic photographs provides today's professionals with models for what will resonate going forward. As humans, we all constantly rely on the visual sense to see changes in the area where we live and work; in turn, the surviving artifacts and the remnants of the past may become more meaningful. Perhaps this is why preservation controversies are such a common land-use theme. As landscape essayist J. B. Jackson informed us long ago, the imagery of ruins inspires us to recreate past glories by starting anew.

6. Iskra Johnson, "Gentrification and Appropriation, the Tagger and the Voyeur: Chinatown in Transition," *Iskra Fine Art* (blog), January 19, 2016, http://iskrafineart.com/gentrification-and-appropriation-the-tagger-and-the-voyeur-chinatown-in-transition/#more-4621.

7. Tyrone Beason, "Put the Smartphone Down and See the World with New Eyes—Your Eyes," *Seattle Times*, February 18, 2016, http://www.seattletimes.com/pacific-nw-magazine/dont-wait-for-the-reviews-rediscover-the-joy-of-exploration/.

8. Finlo Rohrer of BBC News has summarized the messages from many recent books on the virtues of walking as follows:

    - Walk further and with no fixed route.
    - Stop texting and mapping.
    - Don't soundtrack your walks.
    - Go alone.
    - Find walkable places.
    - Walk mindfully.

    See: Finlo Rohrer, "The Slow Death of Purposeless Walking," *BBC News Magazine*, May 1, 2014, http://www.bbc.com/news/magazine-27186709.

9. James A. Clapp, *The City: A Dictionary of Quotable Thoughts on Cities and Urban Life*, 2nd ed. (New Brunswick, NJ: Transaction Publishers, 2014), 14.

10. William Shakespeare, *Coriolanus* 3.1.199, in *The Oxford Shakespeare, The Complete Works*, 2nd ed., ed. Stanley Wells

and Gary Taylor (Oxford: Oxford University Press, 2005), 638.

11. J. B. Jackson, *The Necessity for Ruins, and Other Topics* (Amherst, MA: University of Massachusetts Press, 1980); Lewis Mumford, *The City in History* (New York: Harcourt, Brace & World, 1961).

12. Joseph Rykwert, *The Seduction of Place: The History and Future of Cities* (New York: Vintage Books, 2002).

13. Joseph Rykwert, *The Idea of a Town: The Anthropology of Urban Form in Rome, Italy, and the Ancient World* (Princeton, NJ: Princeton University Press, 1976), 202.

14. John R. Stilgoe, *Outside Lies Magic: Regaining History and Awareness in Everyday Places* (New York: Walker and Co., 1998).

15. Hiss, *The Experience of Place*, 3.

16. Charles Dickens, quoted in: Jon Mee, "Dickens and the City: 'Animate London . . . Inanimate London,'" chap. 3 in *The Cambridge Introduction to Charles Dickens* (Cambridge, UK: Cambridge University Press, 2010), 43.

17. Mee, Ibid., 46.

18. Charles Dickens, *Bleak House* (Oxford: Oxford University Press, 1996), 58. For similar references to the descriptive skills of Dickens (including the opening passage of *Bleak House*), of other authors, and, especially, of later work by James Joyce, see: Mohsen Mostafavi, "Tale of Cities," in *In the Life of Cities*, ed. Mohsen Mostafavi (Zürich: Lars Müller; Cambridge, MA: Harvard University Graduate School of Design, 2012), 7–15.

19. Linda Lappin, *The Soul of Place: Creative Writing Workbook* (Palo Alto, CA: Travelers' Tales, 2015), ch. 2.

20. Luc Sante, *The Other Paris* (London: Macmillan, 2015).

21. Susan Sontag, *On Photography* (New York: Picador, 1990), 55.

22. Greg Bogaerts, *Walking Paris Streets with Eugène Atget: Inspired Stories about the Ragpicker, Lampshade Vendor, and Other Characters and Places of Old France* (Brunswick, ME: Shanti Arts Publishing, 2013), Introduction.

23. See: Rebecca Solnit, *Wanderlust: A History of Walking* (New York: Penguin Books, 2000); Alexandra Horowitz, *On*

Looking: A Walker's Guide to the Art of Observation (New York: Scribner, 2014).

24. Missy Higgins and Dan Lee, interview, September 2015.

25. The song "Going North" comes from Higgins' album *On a Clear Night* (Warner Brothers / Reprise, 2007); Lee's play *Bottomless* is described by the Victoria State Library at: http://www.slv.vic.gov.au/about-us/scholarships-awards /re-ross-trust-playwrights-script-development-awards /dan-william-lee.

26. Timmah Ball, "Last Stone Left: Well-Being and Aboriginal Placemaking in the City," *ASSEMBLE Papers*, October 5, 2015, http://assemblepapers.com.au/2015/10/05/last-stone -left-wellbeing-and-aboriginal-placemaking-in-the-city/).

27. Erin Tam, interview, November 2015.

28. See: David Adjaye, *Adjaye, Africa, Architecture*, ed. Peter Allison (London: Thames and Hudson, 2011).

29. See: Min Li Chan, "Replenishing a Sense of Wonder in Cities," *the polis blog,* April 2014, http://www.thepolisblog .org/2015/11/replenishing-sense-of-wonder-in-cities.html; see also: Gail Jones, *Five Bells* (New York: Picador, 2011).

30. Access the Gail Jones interview at: Writers and Company, "*Five Bells* with Novelist Gail Jones," *CBC player*, December 9, 2012, http://www.cbc.ca/player/play/2313221618.

31. Ibid.; for the archived photos of Sydney published as *Demolition Books*, see: http://www.cityofsydney.nsw.gov.au/learn /search-our-collections.

32. Chan, "Replenishing a Sense of Wonder in Cities."

33. Forebears and insightful texts also include the following, and most are also mentioned elsewhere in the narrative. This is a limited list, and extensive bibliographies are also available from Professor Emeritus Dennis Ryan at the University of Washington, who taught an elective course, "Reading the City," for many years:

    1. Kevin Lynch's iconic characterizations of urban form in *The Image of the City* (Cambridge, MA: MIT Press, 1960) and those of former San Francisco planning director and academic Allan Jacobs in *Looking at Cities* (Cambridge,

MA: Harvard University Press, 1984) are perhaps best known for setting the tone for urban observation from the 1960s through the 1980s.

2. In *American Urban Form: A Representative History* (Cambridge, MA: MIT Press, 2012), Sam Bass Warner and Andrew Whittemore provide an outstanding illustrated history of American urban form via a hypothetical city constructed from the histories of Boston, Philadelphia, and New York City, with the specific goal of understanding the past in order to plan the future. As summarized by MIT Press, the book's depiction of "changing patterns of houses, buildings, streets, parks, pipes and wires, wharves, railroads, highways, and airports reflect changing patterns of the social, political, and economic processes that shape the city." This volume is important in deriving lessons from observation of today's evolving and interdisciplinary urban environments.

3. In *Extacity* (New York: Princeton Architectural Press, 2003), Nigel Coates provides an alternative to the Warner and Whittemore generic model with a nonlinear book that presents an imaginary city in the form of the sensual side of all cities. Coates combines seven cities from around the world into one urban fabric—and provides dynamic visual representations of multiple ways to get to know urban surroundings. *Extacity*'s principles are a gateway to multimedia approaches to urban diaries beyond my photography.

Finally, as noted in the text, Grady Clay's foundational *Close-Up: How to Read the American City* (Chicago: University of Chicago Press, 1980) provides keys to the observation and deciphering of cities, and challenges individuals to discover from their own perspectives.

34. Kevin Lynch and Malcolm Rivkin, "A Walk Around the Block," *Landscape* 8, no. 3 (1959): 24–34.

35. Gordon Cullen, *The Concise Townscape* (London: Architectural Press, 1961).

36. Edmund N. Bacon, *Design of Cities*, rev. ed. (Middlesex, UK: Penguin Books, 1978).

37. Ibid., 57.

38. Anne Mikoleit and Moritz Pürckhauer, *Urban Code: 100 Lessons for Understanding the City* (Cambridge, MA: MIT Press, 2011).

39. For more on historian Paul Dorpat, see: https://pauldorpat .com.

40. For updates and additional detail about the *Ghosts of Seattle Past* project, see: http://www.seattleghosts.com.

41. Jaimee Garbacik, interviews, December 2015 and January 2016.

42. Ibid.

43. Samantha Updegrave, in: Jaimee Garbacik et al., *Ghosts of Seattle Past* (beta draft, January 2016), unpaginated Foreword.

44. Hipstamatic is explained in detail at: http://hipstamatic.com /camera/.

45. For more on the HipstaPak for Hipstamatic, see: http: //hipstography.com/en/news-en/the-manchester-hipstapak -2.html.

46. See the QuizTrail app in action at: http://quiztrail.com.

47. For details on Leica Store City's use of Quiztrail, see: http: //leicarumors.com/2016/01/04/leica-teams-up-with-quiztrail -for-interactive-london-photo-trail.aspx/#more-39013.

48. The Walc app and turn-by-turn navigation appear at: http: //www.walc.me.

49. For additional detail on the Likeways app, see: https: //likeways.wordpress.com.

50. Drift's adaptation of the Situationist approach is explained at: http://www.brokencitylab.org/drift/.

51. For more on the Where in Wally app, see: https://architectse17 .wordpress.com/where-in-wally/.

52. For an explanation of the purpose and goals of Mappiness, see: http://www.mappiness.org.uk. The app was developed by George McKerron, London School of Economics.

53. Marcus Foth, Kelen Klaebe, and Greg Hearn, "The Role of New Media and Digital Narratives in Urban Planning and Community Development" (undated report, Institute for Creative Industries and Innovation, Queensland Univer-

sity of Technology, Brisbane), http://people.brunel.ac.uk
/bst/vol0702/marcusfoth/. See also: https://www.rockefeller
foundation.org/blog/digital-storytelling-social-impact/;
http://civicmediaproject.org/works/civic-media-project
/your-story-goes-here.

54. For Placecheck's gateway website, see: http://www.placecheck
.info.

55. Extensive resources for the Placecheck Walkabout appear
at: http://www.placecheck.info/the-placecheck-walkabout/.

56. A helpful document, "21 Questions for the Placecheck
Walkabout," is downloadable at: http://www.placecheck
.info/wp-content/uploads/2012/03/21-questions-for-the
-Placecheck-walkabout.pdf.

57. For additional prompts, see: http://www.placecheck.info
/wp-content/uploads/2012/03/Extra-prompts-for-the
-Placecheck-walkabout.pdf.

58. For more stories, see: http://www.placecheck.info/placecheck
-stories/.

59. Both Photowalk and Soundwalk were championed by the
virtual City Builder Book Club in 2015:

> Share the sights of your city. Create a photowalk that tells a
> visual story about your neighbourhood or city and the people
> that live there. Through photos and brief descriptions tied to
> map locations, give us a peek into your neighbourhood.
>
> Go for a walk and capture the sights along the way.
> Move through a neighbourhood and take photos of the little
> nuances that make it unique. Take snapshots of the people
> and the places that tell a story about your city. We want to
> see its delightful, troubling, funny, and fleeting moments,
> captured on camera and tied to place.

See: http://citybuilderbookclub.org/2015/02/26/interactive
-activity-your-city-photowalks/.

Photowalk examples have included "A story about
industry and change along the waterfront in Red Hook,
Brooklyn," "A story about everyday urban life in Zagreb,
Croatia," and "A story about gentrification along Toronto's
Queen Street East." Each provided the ability to follow a

mapped route, click on photo icons and read a captioned explanation—essentially a virtual guided tour. Several examples resulted from a Ryerson University course on Global Cities.

Photowalk uses the open-source, publicly accessible Storymap platform created by Northwestern University's Knight Lab; Soundwalk uses the free Audacity sound editor. See: https://citybuilderbookclub.files.wordpress .com/2014/05/cbbc_photowalk_guide.pdf; https://citybuilder bookclub.files.wordpress.com/2014/05/cbbc_soundwalk _guide.pdf.

60. For supplemental information on StoryMap, see: http: //storymap.knightlab.com/.

61. Soundwalk examples include primary, single-instance recordings of a Sao Paulo transit venue and a Toronto sample. While easily augmented with web links, they lack the dynamic, guided progression of Photowalk.

62. Guidance on the urban storytellers' teaching kit appears at: https://urbanstorytellers.makes.org/thimble /MzY3OTE5MTA0/urban-storytelling-a-how-to-guide -start-here.

63. The teaching kit provides some compelling narrative that is not necessarily limited in applicability to the intended audience of "citizen planners":

> The act of creating and sharing stories about specific locations in cities and neighbourhoods empowers citizens to participate in the ongoing urban planning dialogue by adding their insight and lived experiences to the conversation.
>
> Stories, or narratives, play a critically important role in communicating our perspective within our community and to the broader public. An effectively told story can influence decision-makers and spark wider discussions in our cities and neighbourhoods. We are all experts on the subject of where we live, and our stories about places we know and love (or know and want to change) can be an evocative, eloquent, and compelling force for change in urban planning—and elsewhere.

Likewise, the kit language emphasizes imagery as much as words and makes an excellent introductory read for any budding urban diarist:

Citizen planners (that's you!) will create a digital, multimedia story using video, photographs, audio, and anything else you want to use. Using your keywords and your key images, your story will uncover details about a location—a park, a street, a lamp-post, an intersection, a building façade, an empty field, a new development, a favourite passageway—well, you get the picture! By combining your powerful keywords and fantastic images you can create a visual exploration of how cities work for people (or don't), and perhaps show how to make our cities better places to live.

See: https://urbanstorytellers.makes.org/thimble /MzY3OTE5MTA0/urban-storytelling-a-how-to-guide -start-here.

64. A summary of Dawn McDougall's Philly Urban Diary project appears at: https://dawnmcdougall.com/past-work/.

65. For a synopsis of the Corner app, see: http://bigapps.nyc /project/1421/corner-a-local-reporting-mobile-platform.

66. For example, see: Baltimore Urban Diary assignment, developed in spring 2014 for H. Berkeley's course "City in Life and Letters," http://cill2014.blogspot.com/2014/02 /urban-diaries-assignment.html:

One of the key components of our City in Life and Letters class will be the Urban Diaries that we assemble during the course of the semester. We will, on a regular basis, be heading into different parts of the city. Each time we take a trip, you will have a reading in advance that will give you a glimpse into the neighborhood we'll be visiting. You will be responsible for reading the article, developing a list of questions it has raised for you and formulating a plan for how you will use your time in the neighborhood to "answer" your questions. Will you interview residents of the neighborhood? Will you focus your observations on particular aspects of the neighborhood? Which of the fiction and nonfiction readings we've done will you connect to what you see in this neighborhood? Will you document your study with pictures, video, sketches?

Your homework following each trip is to complete an Urban Diary entry, which includes:

1. The list of questions you had generated in advance of the trip.
2. The results of your explorations, in the form of notes and impressions, video, photos, sketches, interviews, observations, etc.
3. Connections between issues and ideas we've read and talked about in class and your experience in the neighborhood.

67. Blogger Kieu Huynh's model urban diary blog and articles appear at: https://urbandiarist.wordpress.com.

Chapter 3 Notes

1. Susan Sontag, *On Photography* (New York: Picador, 1990), 4.
2. Bonnie Yochelson, ed., *Berenice Abbott: Changing New York* (New York: New Press and the Museum of the City of New York, 1997).
3. Terri Weissman, *The Realisms of Berenice Abbott* (Berkeley, CA: University of California Press, 2011). Weissman explains how the passage was part of a letter from Abbott to Charles C. Adams (commonly cited as 1939, but noted as 1929 in the Berenice Abbott Papers, New York Public Library, http://archives.nypl.org/mss/17972#detailed).
4. John Raeburn, "Culture Morphology in Berenice Abbott's New York," in *A Staggering Revolution: A Cultural History of Thirties Photography* (Champaign, IL: University of Illinois Press, 2006), 129.
5. Berenice Abbott, *A Guide to Better Photography* (New York: Crown, 1941), as quoted by John Raeburn, 127.
6. Alexander Cockburn, "Bwana Vistas," *Harper's Magazine*, August 1985, 65–69.
7. Charles R. Wolfe, "Remembrance of Cities Past: Spectacular Photos of the Way We Lived," *Grist*, June 29, 2011, http:

//grist.org/cities/2011-06-28-the-continued-relevance-of
-reclaiming-the-urban-memory/, quoting Burton Holmes
in Seoul, Korea, 1899, courtesy of his biographer, Genoa
Caldwell.

8. Rob Forbes, *See for Yourself: A Visual Guide to Everyday Beauty* (San Francisco: Chronicle Books, 2015); for Forbes's TED Talk, see: https://www.ted.com/talks/rob_forbes_on _ways_of_seeing?language=en.

9. The benefits of a camera over a sketchpad are often cited by Forbes, particularly in *See for Yourself*, 172.

10. George Nelson, *How to See: A Guide to Reading Our Man-Made Environment* (Stamford, CT: Design Within Reach, 2002).

11. Ibid.

12. Ibid., 95.

13. Forbes, *See for Yourself*, 175.

14. Ibid.

15. Anne Whiston Spirn, *The Eye Is a Door* (Georgia, USA: Wolf Tree Press, 2014), e-book available at: http://www .theeyeisadoor.com/#3.

16. See these Ansel Adams quotations and many others assembled at http://www.photoquotes.com/showquotes .aspx?id=10&name=Adams,Ansel.

17. Ansel Adams and Mary Street Alinder, *Ansel Adams: An Autobiography* (New York: Little Brown and Company, 1996), 235.

18. See: "Participatory Photography Partnership Guide, from Community Assessment to Political Action" (Oregon Community Health Partnership, Portland, OR), http://ophi.org /download/PDF/healthy_planning_pdfs/ophi%20photovoice %20guide_0916.pdf.

The helpful hints listed in the guide include:

COMPOSITION

Composition is fundamental in photography. It takes time, effort, practice, and sometimes luck to achieve a well-composed photograph.

When introducing composition, get students to look at the following elements:

- Foreground and background—what is the relationship between them?
- The main subject or focal point—where should it be placed within the frame?
- Cropping within the frame—do you want to include all of the main subject?
- The basic shapes in the picture
- The effect of dividing the frame diagonally
- Creating space between objects
- Proximity or distance from the main subject

HOLDING THE CAMERA STILL

- Encouraging participants to support the camera to ensure that there's no blur

CAMERA ANGLE/POINT OF VIEW

These affect both the composition and the emotional feel of a photograph. Play around with looking down on people and looking up. Encourage participants to use their bodies and their imagination—to crouch, or to stand on chairs, for example. If you are working with children, remember they will always have a different perspective on the world—which can be very interesting.

MOVEMENT

A sense of movement can often make a picture. Composition plays a role here, as the position of a moving subject will influence how it is read. Is the subject moving into or out of the picture? Explain how different settings can be used to capture movement, and encourage the participants to experiment with panning. Look at sport photography as an example—get participants to experiment.

UNDERSTANDING LIGHT

The word *photography* is derived from the Greek and means "drawing with light." It is important to discuss light and its different properties, especially the differences in natural lighting through the day, from early morning to dusk. This will enable participants to decide when to go on outshoot. Also discuss shadows and reflections and how these affect photos.

FLASH PHOTOGRAPHY

Explain the differences between the quality of artificial light and that of natural light, and the use of flash in photography.

LINES, PATTERNS, AND TEXTURES

Encourage participants to look at different textures and patterns and to consider how these can affect a picture and its composition. Encourage them to practice photographing subjects with strong lines.

BUILD YOUR OWN EXERCISES

With all of the elements above, design exercises for students to get used to these concepts, for example:

- Take the same picture from three different angles, to use both horizontal and portrait framing.
- Take three pictures where the background is important.
- Take three pictures that focus on color, three focusing on pattern, line, and texture, etc.
- Create an exercise around movement and allow the participants to experiment with both color and black-and-white photography.

COMMON MISTAKES

Mistakes are an important and inevitable part of the learning process. They include:

- Fingers, hair, or straps over the lens
- Camera shake
- Taking pictures from too far away
- Cutting heads off / unintentional cropping

19. Henry Carroll, *Read This if You Want to Take Great Photographs* (London: Laurence King Publishing, 2014).

20. Richard Conlin, interview, January 2015.

21. Facebook communication by Mike O'Brien, April 2014.

22. John Berger and Jean Mohr, *Another Way of Telling* (New York: Vintage International, 1995), 85.

23. To view the photograph and additional works exhibited at the Harry Ransom Center in the University of Texas at Austin, see: http://www.hrc.utexas.edu/exhibitions/permanent /firstphotograph/#top/.

24. To learn more about the Julia Baier's 2016 workshop "Right Beside You" at Leica Fotografie International, see: http: //lfi-online.de/ceemes/en/workshop/right-beside-you-886 .html.

25. This urban diary role is consistent with the "Finding the Soul of the City" worksheet, compiled by Elizabeth Vander Schaaf for the Louisiana Voices Folklife in Education Project. "We no longer live in a culture that recognizes the soul of a place. We have to do the work ourselves," notes Vander Schaff. See extensive resources at: http://www.louisianavoices .org/Unit4/edu_unit4_lesson3.html#materials and http: //www.louisianavoices.org/Unit4/edu_unit4w_spirit_of _place.html. See also: Elizabeth Vander Schaaf, "Finding the Soul of the City," *Utne Reader*, September/October 1994.

26. Allan Jacobs, *Looking at Cities* (Cambridge, MA: Harvard University Press, 1984).

27. Christopher L. Salter, "How to Read a City: A Geographic Perspective," *OAH Magazine of History* 5, no. 2 (Fall 1990), 68–71.

28. Jacob A. Riis, *How the Other Half Lives: Studies Among the Tenements of New York*, reprint ed. (New York: Dover, 1971). The book was originally published in 1890.

29. A brief history of the Olmsted/Jones technique appeared in: Kathy Mulady, "A Walk in the Park: How It Was All Planned," *Seattle Post-Intelligencer*, April 1, 2003, http://www.seattlepi.com/news/article/A-walk-in-the -park-How-it-was-all-planned-1111156.php. See also: David Williams and Walt Crowley, "John Olmsted Arrives in Seattle to Design City Parks on April 30, 1903,"

HistoryLink, May 20, 2001, http://www.historylink.org /index.cfm?DisplayPage=output.cfm&File_Id=3290.

30. Other early, non-urban examples of a focus on beauty included Carleton Watkins's photographs from the 1860s, which helped save Yosemite. See: Leo Hickman, "Carleton Watkins and the Photographs That Saved Yosemite," *The Guardian*, December 30, 2011.

31. See: Jonathan Raban, *Soft City* (London: Harvill Press, 1974); Kevin Lynch, *The Image of the City* (Cambridge, MA: MIT Press, 1960); and Nigel Coates, *Extacity* (New York: Princeton Architectural Press, 2003).

32. In *The Soul of Place: Creative Writing Workbook* (Palo Alto, CA: Travelers' Tales, 2015), Linda Lappin discusses performance artists Michael Shanks and Mike Pearson's thematic maps, where a "quester" chooses a certain theme, topic or object.

Chapter 4 Notes

1. Charles Beaudelaire, "Miss Scalpel," in *Le Spleen de Paris* (*The French Prowler*), trans. Edward K. Kaplan (Athens, GA: University of Georgia Press, 1997), 15.

2. See: Matthew Carmona, Steve Tiesdell, Tim Heath, and Tanner Oc, *Public Spaces—Urban Spaces* (Oxford, UK: The Architectural Press, 2010), 131.

3. Ibid.

4. See ch. 3, endnote 32.

5. See: Charles R. Wolfe, "Inspiring the Walkable Waterside: Who Gets, Who Pays?" *myurbanist* (blog), July 18, 2010, http://www.myurbanist.com/archives/3384; see also: Charles Wolfe, "Density Stories: Grace in Vertical Space," *myurbanist* (blog), April 13, 2010, http://www.myurbanist .com/archives/2168.

6. See: Charles R. Wolfe, "Shutters, Placemaking, and Urbanism," *myurbanist* (blog), June 13, 2010, http://www.myurbanist .com/archives/2937.

7. Sir Patrick Geddes, *Cities in Evolution: An Introduction to the Town Planning Movement and to the Study of Civics* (London: Williams & Norgate, 1915).

8. See generally: Miles Glendinning, *The Conservation Movement: A History of Architectural Preservation* (Abington, UK: Routledge, 2013).

9. Gordon Cullen, *The Concise Townscape* (London: Architectural Press, 1961).

10. Edmund N. Bacon, *Design of Cities*, rev. ed. (Middlesex, UK: Penguin Books, 1978).

11. Charles R. Wolfe, "Movement and Settlement, Upside Down," *myurbanist* (blog), April 19, 2013, http://www.myurbanist.com/archives/9685.

12. Berenice Abbott, *A Guide to Better Photography* (New York: Crown, 1941).

13. See, for example: Hal Dardinck, "Daley Took Out Loans to Run Millennium Park," *Chicago Tribune*, November 14, 2013, http://articles.chicagotribune.com/2013-11-04/news/ct-met-daley-millennium-park-1105-20131105_1_cloud-gate-sculpture-daley-debt-payments.

14. See: Charles R. Wolfe, "What Is Trespass in the City?" *myurbanist* (blog), June 19, 2010, http://www.myurbanist.com/archives/3002.

15. See: Charles R. Wolfe, "Reading the Evolution of Places," *myurbanist* (blog), August 22, 2010, http://www.myurbanist.com/archives/3764.

16. See: William H. Whyte, *The Social Life of Small Urban Spaces* (New York: Project for Public Spaces, 2001); Jan Gehl and Birgitte Svarre, *How to Study Public Life* (Washington, DC: Island Press, 2013).

17. Leonard Pitt, *Paris: A Journey Through Time* (Berkeley, CA: Counterpoint, 2010).

18. Ibid., unpaginated introduction.

19. Ibid.

Chapter 5 Notes

1. Nan Ellin, "The Tao of Urbanism," in *What We See: Advancing the Observations of Jane Jacobs*, ed. Stephen A. Goldsmith and Lynne Elizabeth (Oakland, CA: New Village Press, 2010), 52.

2. Mohsen Mostafavi, "Tale of Cities," in *In the Life of Cities*, ed. Mohsen Mostafavi (Zürich: Lars Müller; Cambridge, MA: Harvard University Graduate School of Design, 2012), 15.

3. Braided River explains its approach and associated books, exhibits, and events at: http://www.braidedriver.org.

4. Heart Foundation, "Neighborhood Walkability Checklist," 2011, https://heartfoundation.org.au/images/uploads/main/Active_living/Neighbourhood-walkability-checklist.pdf.

5. See: chapter 2, notes 53–63.

6. See: Marc Kushner, "A New Golden Age of Architecture," March 10, 2015, https://medium.com/@marchitizer/a-new-golden-age-of-architecture-825fb7ed652c.

7. Ibid.

8. For viewing a selection of Marc Kushner's talks, see: https://www.ted.com/talks/marc_kushner_why_the_buildings_of_the_future_will_be_shaped_by_you; also, see: Marc Kushner, "Form No Longer Follows Function, It Works with It," https://vimeo.com/128494365; and: "Architecture Is Undergoing a Democratic Revolution," http://www.psfk.com/2015/05/architizer-ceo-marc-kushner-architecture-democratic-revolution.html.

9. See: Francesca Perry, "Lagos on Instagram: From Selling Bubblegum to Cycling in the Sun," *The Guardian*, February 26, 2016, http://www.theguardian.com/cities/2016/feb/26/lagos-on-instagram-from-selling-bubblegum-to-cycling-in-the-sun.

10. For more details regarding this event, see: http://www.whatdoyoupicture.ca/; see also: http://vancouver.ca/home-property-development/neighbourhood-planning-projects.aspx.

11. See: Corelia Barbarac, "The 'Urban Spacebook' Experimental Process: Co-designing a Platform for Participation," *Journal of Community Informatics* 10, no. 3 (2014), http://ci-journal.net/index.php/ciej/article/view/1129/1119.

12. See, for example: Kirsten Howard, "NH Citizens and Photographers Invited to Participate in King Tide Photo Contest Wednesday at Noon," *NH Coastal Adaptation Workgroup*

Blog, October 27, 2015, http://ci-journal.net/index.php/ciej
/article/view/1129/1119); see also: http://nhblog.stormsmart
.org/nh-citizens-and-photographers-invited-to-participate
-in-king-tide-photo-contest-wednesday-at-noon/.

13. For Boston app, see: http://www.cityofboston.gov/doit
/apps/311.asp; for Philadelphia app, see: http://www.phila
.gov/311/Pages/default.aspx.

14. To learn more about Austin's thirty-year Imagine Austin
plan, see: http://www.austintexas.gov/department/about
-imagine-austin.

15. For details regarding Austin's CodeNEXT initiative, see:
http://austintexas.gov/codenext.

16. For a list of frequently answered questions regarding Austin's "Community Character in a Box" toolkit, see: http:
//www.austintexas.gov/sites/default/files/files/Planning
/CodeNEXT/Community_Character_in_a_Box_FAQ1
.pdf.

17. For a digital brochure of Austin's "Community Character in
a Box" toolkit, see: https://www.austintexas.gov/sites
/default/files/files/Planning/CodeNEXT/CODENEXT
-CCB-PART-11x17-HANDOUT_v5-13-14_Revised.pdf.

18. To view a compilation of event photos from CodeNEXT,
see: https://www.flickr.com/photos/119725136@N06/sets.

19. See: Phoebe Crisman, "Outside the Frame: A Critical
Analysis of Urban Image Surveys," *Places* 16, no. 2 (2006).
See also: http://www.people.virginia.edu/~pc4v/pdf/Crisman
_Outside_the_Frame_Places_07.pdf.

20. Caroline Wang and Mary Ann Burris, "Photovoice: Concept, Methodology, and Use for Participatory Needs Assessment," *Health Education & Behavior* 24, no. 3 (1997): 369.

21. Photovoice resources include: Ricardo da Silva Vieria and
Paula Antunes, "Using Photo-Surveys to Inform Participatory Urban Planning Processes: Lessons from Practice,"
Land Use Policy 38 (2014), 497–508 and: Amelia Brown,
"Photography & Participation: How Photovoice Engages
and Rebuilds Communities, *Creative Exchange*, May 21,
2015, http://www.springboardexchange.org/features/photo
voice.aspx.

22. See: Debra Webb, "Placemaking and Social Equity, Expanding the Framework of Creative Placemaking," *Activate, a Journal of Entrepreneurship and the Arts* 3, no. 1 (2014), 35–48. The leaders of the Yesler Terrace photovoice project included Claire Garoutte, of Seattle University's fine arts department; Asfaha Lemlem, coordinator of Yesler Terrace RechTec Computer Lab and Learning Center; Kat Vellos, program director at Youth in Focus; and Assaye Abunie, executive director of the Multimedia Resource and Training Institute.

23. To view student work from the Yesler Terrace Youth Media project, see: http://ytyouthmedia.com.

24. Webb, "Placemaking and Social Equity," 44.

25. Ibid., 45.

26. To learn about the California King Tides Project's 2014 flood risk documentation, see: http://california.kingtides .net/plan/our-coast-our-future/.

27. To learn more about WALKscope's data collection process, see: http://www.walkscope.org/tips/.

28. "Precedent Mini-Case: Bryant Park, New York City, NY," in *Places in the Making: How Placemaking Builds Places and Communities* (White Paper, Department of Urban Studies and Planning, Massachusetts Institute of Technology, 2013), https://dusp.mit.edu/sites/dusp.mit.edu/files/attachments /project/mit-dusp-places-in-the-making.pdf.

29. Charles Arthur, "Google Buys Neural Network City Guide Creator Jetpac," *The Guardian*, August 18, 2014, https: //www.theguardian.com/technology/2014/aug/18/google -buys-neural-network-city-guide-creator-jetpac.

30. See: Charles Arthur, "Instagram Pictures Reveal Belfast as the UK's Happiest City," *The Guardian*, January 13, 2014, https://www.theguardian.com/technology/2014/jan/13 /instagram-pictures-belfast-uk-happiest-city-jetpac.

31. Ibid.

32. For a summary of Cesar Hidalgo's empirical work at the MIT Media Lab, as well as studies by Marco De Nadai and Bruno Lepri, see: Kelsey Campbell-Dollaghan, "What a Neural Network Thinks About Your Neighborhood—And

Why It Matters," *FastCompany Co-Design*, August 9, 2016, http://www.fastcodesign.com/3062516/what-a-neural -network-thinks-about-your-neighborhood-and-why-it -matters.

33. Researchers increasingly study uploaded and aggregated Instagram photographs to derive conclusions about human behavior and wealth distribution. See: Linda Poon, "Donating Your Selfies to Science," *CityLab*, February 16, 2016, http://www.citylab.com/tech/2016/02/photo-share -social-media-instagram-google-street-view-urban-life -airtick/462495/; see also: Linda Poon, "What Instagram Reveals About Inequality in New York City," *CityLab*, July 27, 2016, http://www.citylab.com/tech/2016/07 /what-instagram-reveals-about-inequality-in-new-york -city/493046/.

34. For more on the AirTick app, see: http://www.nrf.gov.sg /gyss-one-north/gyss@one-north-2016/singapore-challenge /singapore-challenge-2016-finalists/jedi-pan-zheng -xiang.

35. To read about Abbotsford's community-engagement work through the Abbotsforward initiative, visit: http://www .abbotsford.ca/business_and_development/major_initiatives /abbotsforward_ocp_update.htm#Stage2.

36. For a compilation of data collection methods from the Abbotsforward initiative, see: https://www.abbotsford.ca /Assets/2014+Abbotsford/Planning+and+Development /OCP+Update/Abbotsforward+Background+Research+Re port+-+Appendix+A.pdf.

37. To learn more about how the Adelaide engaged community members through the Picture Adelaide 2040 initiative, see: http://pictureadelaide.com.au.

38. For a summary of activities and results from the Picture Adelaide 2040 initiative, see: http://pictureadelaide.com.au /user_assets/0e5873a230b49cc8d6c48effb610693d733a069d /pa2040.pdf.

39. To view a summary of Albany 2030's public outreach efforts and results, see: http://www.albany2030.org/files/sites /default/files/Appendix%20B_PublicOutreach.pdf.

40. To learn more about how San Jose used the Wikiplanning online tool as part of a civic engagement campaign, see: https://www.sanjoseca.gov/DocumentCenter/View/3336.

41. Elena Umanskaya, "Public Participation in Historic Preservation Planning: Engaging the Community into Planning for Redmond's Historic Core," University of Washington, CEP Senior Project, 2014, 29.

42. Ibid., 30.

43. "Walk, Talk, and Explore Redmond's Old Town Historic Core," *Redmond Reporter*, May 31, 2014, http://www.redmond-reporter.com/community/261299841.html.

44. For a detailed workbook of Redmond's "Walk & Talk & Nuts & Bolts" workshop, see: http://www.redmond.gov/common/pages/UserFile.aspx?fileId=128441.

45. Interview with Kim Dietz, March 2016.

46. For a list of recent planning topics under review by the City of Redmond, see: http://www.redmond.gov/cms/One.aspx?portalId=169&pageId=556.

47. To read a list of community-based outcomes from Melbourne's Central City Urban Forest planning effort, see: http://participate.melbourne.vic.gov.au/application/files/9314/1273/6913/Central_City_Urban_Forest_Consultation_Outcomes.pdf.

48. Murphy McCullough, interview, March 2016.

49. See, for example: "Central District Discusses 23rd Ave Business Support," *Capitol Hill Times*, March 16, 2016, http://www.capitolhilltimes.com/2016/03/central-district-discusses-23rd-ave-business-support/.

50. For more on the DRiVEdecisions real estate online tool, see: https://drivedecisions.com.

51. Randolph T. Hester, *Design for Ecological Democracy* (Cambridge, MA: MIT Press, 2010), 7.

52. Ibid., 420.

53. See: Lindsey Collins and Kendra L. Smith, "Empowered Design, by 'The Crowd,'" *Planetizen*, March 17, 2016, http://www.planetizen.com/node/85008/empowered-design-crowd.

54. Ryan Smolar, "BOTTOM UP," *Smolarcorp,* April 20, 2015, http://smolarcorp.weebly.com/blog/bottom-up.
55. Ibid.
56. Sally Clark, interview, November 2015.
57. For Seattle flickr photos, see: https://www.flickr.com /photos/30516210@N02/collections/.
58. For additional detail about the Seattle design-review process, see:

    http://www.seattle.gov/dpd/aboutus/whoweare/designreview /designguidelines/default.htm; http://www.seattle.gov/dpd/cs/groups/pan/@pan/documents /web_informational/p2402708.pdf; http://www.seattle.gov/dpd/cs/groups/pan/@pan/documents /web_informational/dpds021441.pdf; http://www.seattle.gov/dpd/cs/groups/pan/@pan/documents /web_informational/dpds021442.pdf.

59. Daniel G. Parolek, Karen Parolek, and Paul C. Crawford, *Form-Based Codes: A Guide for Planners, Urban Designers, and Developers* (Hoboken, NJ: John Wiley & Sons, 2008), 123.
60. For more on the reinventer.paris design competition see: http://www.reinventer.paris/en/home/.
61. For recent updates on the work of reinventer.paris participants, see: http://www.reinventer.paris/en/meet-up/.
62. Feargus O'Sullivan, "A High-Stakes Contest to 'Reinvent Paris' Fails to Impress," *CityLab*, February 8, 2016, http:// www.citylab.com/design/2016/02/reinventing-paris-winner -jean-louis-missika-anne-hidalgo/460425/.

INDEX

Raleigh, 15–16
Read This if You Want to Take Great Photographs (Carroll), 69–70
Redmond
 city planning by, 162–163
 Historic Core of, 161
 observation of, 26
 photography of, 163–164
 public outreach by, 161
 Redmond palette of, 163f
 urban diary of, 163
reinventer.paris project, 174–175
Reykjavík, 124, p8
Rickard, Doug, 141
riverfront district, p26
Rivkin, Malcolm, 2–3
Roman amphitheater, 119–120, 120f
Rome, 108–109, 108f, p5
Royal Mile, 109, 110f
Rykwert, Joseph
 on human opportunities, 36–37
 The Seduction of Place by, 22–23

Salter, Christopher, 77
Sante, Luc, 3, 39
scale
 for design review, 123
 "incongruity" of, 124
 urban diary and, 169
Seattle, p12
 Cambodian émigrés fishing in, 43–44
 Google Street View of, 141–142, 141f
 Greenwood neighborhood of, 94–95, 95f

Jones, P., photographing of, 81
 juxtaposition of, p22
 Lake Washington in, 91–93, p3
 Madrona neighborhood of, 91
 narrow European streets for, 95, 96f, 97
 nongovernmental organizations of, 144
 Olmsted photographing of, 81
 personal photo of, 141–142, 142f
 photographs of, 17
 skyline of, p2
 transition of, xiii
Seattle Public Library, 8, 8f
The Seduction of Place (Rykwert), 22–23
See for Yourself (Forbes), 64
seeing
 See for Yourself on, 64
 photographs for, 60
 subjectivity of, 63, 65
self-criticism, 72
sensing
 emotional and intellectual responses from, xi
 high priority of, 23, 181
 intentional design influence on, 24
 by Native Americans, 5
 personal experience of, 24
"serial vision"
 of Corsican, 47f
 by Cullen, 47, 116
Sherrard, Jean, 49
simultaneous perception
 The Experience of Place on, 37
 by Hiss, 34